ezard

with teage ezard

photography by ned meldrum

Hardie Grant Books

This edition published in 2004

First published in 2003

by Hardie Grant Books

12 Claremont Street

South Yarra, Victoria 3141,

Australia

www.hardiegrant.com.au

National Library of Australia

Cataloguing-in-Publication Data:

Ezard, Teage.

Ezard: contemporary Australian food.

Includes index.

ISBN 1 74066 185 0.

1. Cookery, Australian. I. Title.

641.5994

Edited by Lucy Malouf

Photographs by Ned Meldrum

Cover and text design by

Hamish Freeman and Klarissa Pfisterer

Typeset by Hamish Freeman and Klarissa Pfisterer

Printed and bound in Singapore by Imago Productions

10 9 8 7 6 5 4 3 2 1

I would like to dedicate this book to my late mother for all of her wonderful meals and to all young cooks starting out – you are the ones that will keep this industry at its very best, for now and forever

Acknowledgements

First and foremost I would like to thank my father for all his help and advice and all the opportunities he has given me. This has been a life-long benefit and I don't think I would be where I am today if it hadn't been for his efforts to teach me about hard work and perseverance, as well as being true to my own instincts. There are many people who contributed in significant ways to putting this book together. I would particularly like to thank the following people: Dane Clouston, who helped me with the framework for the book and who did such a great job testing the recipes. All the members of my kitchen crew, both past and present. In particular, thanks to Ben Cooper, Greg Egan, Chris Donnellan, Alex Delly, Steven Jurisic, Gerard Timmermans and Dylan Verhees. Not just for helping test the recipes, but for the magic they make in the restaurant kitchen every day. A special thanks must go to my head chef and good friend, Brendan McQueen. He did a fabulous job helping me keep it together by organising the team, ordering ingredients, assisting with the photo shoot – and generally making sure that the kitchen kept running seamlessly when I was glued to my computer. Thanks also to my front-of-house team: Luke Stringer, Jane Thornton, Bethanie Ereaut, Chris Kloss, Marcus Stokkel, Samantha Friend and Meredith Stone. I've been really lucky to have had the opportunity of working with the team at Hardie Grant Books. I am particularly grateful to Tracy O'Shaughnessy for being so patient with me and for all her encouragement along the way. I'd also like to thank Lucy Malouf for her invaluable contributions to this book. I simply would not have been able to do it without her. Pam Bakes has been a long-time friend and supporter of all that I do in my cooking. She has an uncanny understanding of what my food is all about, and what I am aiming to achieve with each dish. Her feedback and input along the way have been incredibly helpful. Thanks too, to Ned Meldrum for his amazing photographs and to designers Hamish Freeman and Klarissa Pfisterer, who have made the book look so stunning. On a personal note, I'd like to take the opportunity of thanking my brother Justin for his continuing input to ezard restaurant and also to Tracey for her great support behind the scenes. And finally, to my two favourite little girls, Madeleine and Georgia, thank you for always melting my heart.

ezard

at adelphi

e

contents

introduction

I grew up in the southern suburbs of Melbourne, where I lived with my mother and brother. My mum was a fantastic cook and a great influence on me. Her approach to cooking was that of an artist. She used recipe books as a guide and then tended to do her own thing anyway! But her creative approach to cooking most influenced my own interest in food and cooking, as I could see how much she enjoyed herself.

My cooking career began in 1982 when I was 16 years old. My first job was working at a local hotel in a bayside suburb of Melbourne. It was a really hot summer and the thing I remember most about the experience was how hard I worked and how little cooking I did!

My duties as a kitchen apprentice for an entire year involved the following: cleaning the hotel car park, emptying grease-traps, lugging rubbish bins around the place, kegging beer, painting and maintenance, mopping floors and, of course, washing mountains of dirty dishes. Every week I worked around 80 hours and received the princely sum of $106. The only actual food-handling I did in that first year was peeling carrots and crumbing bits of seafood for the fisherman's baskets.

When I look back, I realize how lucky I was to be working with people who took me under their wing and guided me through that first make-or-break year. Without their interest and support things would have been even tougher.

People often ask me about how my cooking 'style' evolved. I guess the truth is that when it comes to food I have always been driven by drama, excitement and a passion for contrasts. I certainly inherited my mother's artistic flair, and her love of being creative when it comes to putting colours, textures and flavours together on a plate. But more to the point, I have never really been one for following rules and so was never keen to follow the normal path in my cooking career. Many of the cooks I did my apprenticeship with are still cooking the sort of dishes they learned in their training. I couldn't wait to get out there and do my own thing. My style of cooking is not something I learned in school. It is something that has just happened over time.

Of course this experimental style of cooking leads to lots of 'misses' as well as 'hits'. In the early days when I first ran my own kitchen, my head was brimming with ideas and I was constantly dreaming up new dishes. I was really lucky to work with like-minded people at Guernica restaurant, where I was encouraged to let my creative spirit go – and it often ran wild!

The benefit of all this playing around meant that I learned a huge amount about food in terms of what things work well together, and why. This knowledge underpins the way I put dishes together today. I was particularly fortunate too, in that I was able to travel a great deal in my twenties, and this really sparked my interest in Asian cooking.

One of the things I really love about the cuisines of South East Asia is that there are no boundaries. I love the way similar ideas and techniques crop up in different countries around this huge region, but they are often interpreted in very different ways. I find this incredibly appealing and it mirrors my own approach to food and cooking. I am constantly travelling to places like Hong Kong, Indonesia and Thailand, and every time I visit I learn something new and exciting.

My mentor is the legendary chef Mr Hermann Schneider. He is the 'measuring stick' for all that I aspire to in my own career as a chef. As a young apprentice cook I was extremely fortunate to gain a position in his kitchen at Two Faces in the Melbourne suburb of South Yarra, and it was he who instilled in me a passion for the job and a sense of pride in my work. In the tough and chaotic world of restaurant kitchens discipline and true leadership are critical to ensure things run smoothly and to bring out the best in people. And that is exactly the sort of leadership that Mr Schneider provided.

my food philosophy

At ezard, our approach to the preparation and service of food and wine is entirely founded on excellence. Our standards are very high and discipline is a key part of the kitchen. We want to provide the best for our customers so we have to be the best ourselves – our cooks are trained to work with passion and dedication, to use the very best ingredients and to put the best of themselves into the food they are cooking.

I believe that the quality of the produce used in a dish contributes at least 70 percent to the success of the finished product. If you use second-rate ingredients, the result will always be mediocre – and as a cook it's hard to be excited by poor quality produce, so it's unlikely your heart will be in the dish. But if you select the very best, it will inspire you! This, for me, is the important first rule of cooking: choose the best ingredients that are available.

That also means being sensitive to the seasons. Many products are really only at their best in their proper season – a tomato in winter, for instance, has only one use in my view, as a golf ball! Remember that paying top dollar for out-of-season produce doesn't make economic sense, either. We have to be conscious of the cost of things in the restaurant, and I'm sure most home cooks have to be as well. In Australia we are lucky to have a great climate and so can supply a fantastic range of seasonal produce.

As will be clear from the recipes in this book, I'm all for experimentation in the kitchen, rather than always rigidly sticking to tried and tested approaches. Experimentation is what builds confidence in a cook. It's only by trying to do something new that you really learn. Cooking, really, is all about learning from your mistakes.

Knowing when you have made a mistake and understanding why something doesn't work is an essential step on the road to becoming an accomplished cook. We endorse this method in the kitchen at ezard – not just for the benefit of each individual chef's education, but so that mistakes can be identified before a dish gets put in front of a paying customer!

Good original cooking comes from both the heart and the mind. It's worth taking the time to think about the way that different flavours and textures come together in a dish. Being inventive needs more than just imagination and flair – it also needs an understanding of the ingredients and the way things work together. But dishes that have been carefully thought through have the power to excite and inspire. This is what we aim to do at ezard for our customers. This is what my mother used to do for me.

cooking equipment

Many of my recipes are influenced by the culinary traditions of South East Asian cuisines, and as such I employ a wide range of traditional Asian cooking equipment. Luckily, many of these things are readily available in Asian grocery stores, and they tend to be fairly inexpensive. Asian stores are also good places to shop for Asian crockery. I have many bowls and spoons that I use all the time for serving my food, which I think really enhances its presentation.

Historically, these cuisines depended heavily on charcoal-grilling or stove-top cooking (ovens are still relatively scarce in South East Asian kitchens). Cooking methods, therefore, involve boiling, steaming, stir-frying and deep-frying rather than roasting, and cooking utensils reflect this.

I do urge you to buy at least a few of the following items that I consider essential.

wok

If you buy nothing else, please buy a wok! This is one of the most useful and versatile tools in the kitchen. Traditionally it is used for stir-frying, deep-frying, dry-frying, steaming and toasting ingredients. The shape of the wok, with its curved base, means that heat is distributed evenly over its surface, ensuring the intense heat and rapid cooking that is the key to stir-frying.

I suggest that you purchase a mildsteel wok – not a non-stick version – together with a wok spoon for stirring and serving.

All woks need to be 'seasoned'. To season a wok, rub the inside all over with a little cooking oil and heat the wok gently for about 10–15 minutes. Wipe thoroughly with kitchen paper, which will come away blackened. Repeat this process of oiling, heating and wiping until the kitchen paper wipes clean. As you use it, your wok will become darker and well-seasoned.

Never ever wash your wok with soapy water. After each use, wash it in hot water and dry thoroughly before putting it away.

saucepans

The normal range of saucepans found in most home kitchens will suffice for the recipes in this book, but a 5 litre (10 pint) stockpot will make life easier when preparing stocks and soups. A non-reactive (i.e. not aluminium) saucepan is essential for cooking acidic foods. Choose enamel, non-stick or stainless steel.

bamboo steamers

I have a huge number of round bamboo steaming baskets and lids in the restaurant kitchen that I use for steaming food over woks. Bamboo baskets are really cheap and are incredibly versatile. They come in a wide variety of sizes, so will happily accommodate all sorts of food. Also, they stack on top of each other, which means as many as four or five dishes can be steamed simultaneously.

electric rice cooker

This is one modern appliance that has been widely adopted by Asian cooks, and I can't imagine cooking rice without one! They make cooking rice incredibly easy and keep it warm throughout the meal. Another bonus is that a rice cooker keeps the stove top free for cooking other dishes. Rice cookers steam the rice and the result is always evenly cooked and fluffy.

mortar and pestle

These are essential items for grinding spices and herbs and to make wet and dry pastes and spice mixes. They come in all shapes and sizes, made from a variety of materials such as granite, stone and clay. Each South East Asian country has its own preference. My recommendation as a good all-purpose mortar and pestle would be one of the large granite ones.

electric grinders

Grinding spices and herbs by hand is hard work. While I believe that you always get a better texture using a mortar and pestle, there are times when it just is easier to whiz up large amounts in an electric grinder. I find a small coffee grinder works well for largish amounts of dried herbs and spices. Wet pastes can be made in a food processor or electric blender, although I don't think the resulting texture is as good. You do need to make sure that you use a blender or blending attachment with blades that sit flat on the base of the container, otherwise the ingredients will never be properly mixed together.

knives and cleavers

The usual selection of sharp knives will probably be adequate for preparing most South East Asian dishes. I do recommend a small sharp vegetable knife and a vegetable peeler, as well as a heavy cook's knife. Also, no self-respecting Asian cook would be without a large cleaver. These are used for all kinds of cutting, shredding and crushing as well as making light work of bones.

slicers and graters

One of my favourite pieces of kitchen equipment is a Japanese hand-slicer called a binriner. This is a precision tool that is really good for slicing food very finely. I use it for everything from ginger and garlic to sweet potato, carrots, taro, daikon etc. Graters are also useful in the kitchen. In addition to the standard four-sided version that most of us have, I also have a small nutmeg grater, a ginger grater and a special coconut grater I got in Bali. Coconut graters are the key to making your own coconut milk and they are available from specialist catering suppliers. I have to say, though, that nothing beats the simple grater I buy whenever I visit Bali. It is essentially a piece of wood studded with fine nails, and works magic when it comes to grating the flesh of coconuts to a fine, dust-like powder.

cookie cutters

They might seem strange items to have in an Asian-influenced kitchen, but I use these all the time for making hand-made pasta. I have a selection of cutters of different sizes – when I make dumplings I tend to use a smaller cutter to shape the filling neatly and gently under the pasta. It is then easy to seal the dumplings firmly and cut out a neat circle using a larger size cutter.

blow torch

This might seem like something of a luxury item, mainly used by restaurant chefs, but I think the little butane-fuelled blow torches that are readily available these days are a really handy addition to any kitchen. If you like making desserts then I do suggest you buy one – they are essential for producing crème brulées and other caramelised desserts.

special ingredients

banana leaves

These are often used to wrap items for baking over charcoal or for steaming. They add a subtle flavour of their own to a dish. Food served on banana leaves also looks very attractive.

black vinegar

A dark, strong-flavoured vinegar usually made from glutinous rice. It is particularly popular in northern China.

bonito flakes

Used in Japanese cooking. Steamed bonito fish are dried and flaked. They are often mixed with konbu seaweed to form the all-purpose stock, dashi.

dashi

Often available as instant dashi powder. This is an essential stock used in much Japanese cooking. It is made from konbu seaweed and dried bonito.

enoki mushrooms

Thin, white Japanese mushrooms with a round bobble-like head. They have a mildly citrus flavour and are readily available fresh.

fish sauce

A dark, pungent salty sauce made from fermented fish. Known as nuoc mam in Vietnam and nam pla in Thailand.

galangal

An essential ingredient in South East Asian cuisines. Galangal is a rhizome, and a member of the ginger family. Its distinctive flavour is quite different, though, and ginger will not do as a substitute. It is best used fresh.

ghee

Clarified butter, readily available from Asian grocers.

kaffir lime leaves

Dark glossy leaves from a variety of lime tree found throughout South East Asia. The leaves (and sometimes the skin) are most often used in Thai cooking. They have an aromatic citrus flavour. Use only fresh kaffir lime leaves in salads. Frozen leaves are readily available, and, at a pinch, will do for pastes and marinades.

lemongrass

A tall, scented stalk used extensively in Thai and Malaysian cooking. The outer leaves are discarded and the tender, white bottom part of the stalk only is very finely sliced before using.

lotus root

A starchy white root with a crisp texture, that is retained when cooked. Lotus roots have a slightly sweet and pleasingly nutty flavour and are delicious sliced finely and deep-fried into 'crisps'.

mirin

A sweet rice wine used in Japanese cooking. Japanese brands are usually the best quality.

nori

Dried sheets of pressed seaweed. Nori is usually lightly toasted before using as a garnish or for wrapping sushi rolls.

palm sugar

A very hard and distinctively flavoured sugar made from boiling the sap of the sugar palm tree. It has a deep, treacle-like flavour and is used extensively in South East Asian cooking. Versions from Thailand, Indonesia and Malaysia are all readily available. Light and dark versions are used in this book.

pandan leaves

Also known as 'screwpine' leaves. They are used in Thailand, Malaysia and Indonesia for their distinctive flavour and also for their green colour. They are particularly suited to desserts, but are also used to scent boiled rice and curries.

pomegranate molasses

A thick sweet-sour syrup made from boiling down the juice of pomegranates. It is commonly used in Iran and in some other Middle Eastern countries.

rice flour

A very finely ground flour used in Asian cooking. Noodles made from rice flour are silky and smooth with a soft mild flavour.

rice-stick noodles

Dried, semi-translucent noodles made from rice flour. They range in size, but are typically about 2–3 mm (⅛ in) wide and need to be boiled or soaked before use. They are particularly popular in Thailand and Vietnam.

rice-wine vinegar

A traditional Japanese vinegar made from rice wine. Probably best known as the vinegar used to season sushi rice. It is very pale yellow with a subtle, slightly sweet yet clean-tasting flavour.

sake

A Japanese clear wine made from fermented rice. Sake has a high alcohol content (about 16 percent) and is usually drunk warm. The best quality sakes, however, should be drunk chilled.

shiitake mushrooms

Also known as Chinese mushrooms, these are flat, dark brown mushrooms with a firm texture and rich flavour. Fresh shiitake mushrooms are increasingly available, but they are more commonly bought dried, in which case they need to be soaked before use.

shao xing wine

A strong-flavoured Chinese rice wine, mainly used in cooking. You can substitute sherry, at a pinch.

shiso leaf

Also known as Japanese basil or perilla, shiso belongs to the same family as basil and mint, but its flavour is much milder. Shiso leaves are often used as a garnish or can be deep-fried in tempura batter.

sichuan peppercorns

Not related to ordinary black pepper, Sichuan peppercorns are the seeds from the peppery ash tree (fagara). They are most commonly used in Chinese cooking and have a prickly, tingly flavour.

somen noodles

Fine Japanese noodles made from hard wheat dough. They are traditionally eaten cold, although they are sometimes served in a warm broth.

sumac

Commonly used in the Middle East, sumac is a deep rusty-red, coarse powder made from the ground berries of the sumac tree, native to some Mediterranean countries. It has a distinctive sour flavour, and is often used as a condiment or garnish.

tamarind

Extracted from the pods of tamarind trees, and compressed into dark-brown sticky blocks. Tamarind is used as a souring agent in Asian cooking. Tamarind pulp is soaked in water and the juice strained off to produce tamarind water.

tobbiko

Also known as wasabi flying fish roe. Used in Japanese cooking.

turmeric

A rhizome, related to the ginger family. When dried it becomes a vivid yellow colour, and is probably best known for the colour it adds to Indian curry powders. In South East Asia it is commonly used fresh as a vegetable.

wasabi

Also known as Japanese horseradish, although it is unrelated to European horseradish. Fresh wasabi root is virtually impossible to find outside Japan, but it is readily available as pale green powder or ready-mixed paste. It is best to buy it in powder form and use it as required to make the pungent green paste used to accompany sushi and sashimi.

wonton skins

Small square-shaped sheets of fresh dough used to make wonton dumplings and some yum cha dumplings.

yellow rock sugar

Large crystals of yellow-tinged sugar used in Chinese cooking. Readily available from Asian grocers.

conversion tables

Please observe the usual rules when converting between metric and imperial measurements, i.e. never switch between the two systems in the same recipe. Most people these days use the metric system of measurement, and in my view, my recipes work best if cooked using metric measurements. If you are still using the imperial system then please remember that all conversions are approximate, in other words, quantities are rounded up or down.

weights

Grams	Ounces
5	1 teaspoon
10	2 teaspoons
15	½
20	¾
25–30	1
40	1½
60	2
75	3
100	3½
110	4
125	4½
150	5
200	7
250	9
300	10½
350	12
400	14
500 (0.5kg)	16 (1 lb)
1 kg	2 lb
1.5 kg	3 lb

oven temperatures

Celsius	Fahrenheit
120	245
140	280
150	300
160	325
180	350
190	375
200	400
220	425
230	450
240	475

volumes

	Millilitres	Fluid Ounces
	5	1 teaspoon
	10	2 teaspoons
1 tablespoon (UK/US)	15	½
1 tablespoon (Aus)	20	¾
	25–30	1
	40	1½
¼ metric cup	60	2
	75	3
	100	3½
½ metric cup	125	4½
	150	5
	200	7
1 metric cup	250	9
	300	10
	400	13
	*500	16 (1 US pint)
	1 litre	1¾ pints
	2 litres	4 pints

* 1 UK pint = 20 fl oz

dimensions

Centimetres	Inches
5 mm	¼
10 mm (1 cm)	½
2	¾
2.5	1
3	1½
5	2
10	5
15	6
20	8
30	12
40	16
50	20

cook's notes

You can learn more about the specialist ingredients used in the recipes in this book in the Special Ingredients section. A few other things to bear in mind when cooking my recipes are:

Eggs are always free-range and weigh about 63 g (2 oz).

Butter is unsalted.

Milk is full cream.

Cream is either pure (45 percent butterfat) or thickened (35 percent butterfat).

Sugar, in the main, will be specified as caster (superfine) sugar or palm sugar. I mainly use grated light palm sugar for dressings and some desserts. I use dark palm sugar for cooking.

Chocolate is the best quality available. I prefer to use Callebaut or Fortina chocolate, both of which are available from specialist food suppliers.

In the main I use three types of soy sauce in my cooking: a Japanese soy sauce, also known as tamari; a Taiwanese brand of light soy sauce and an Indonesian brand of sweet soy sauce, also known as ketjap manis.

I prefer to use salt flakes for their quality and mild flavour. Avoid iodised table salts if possible.

Pepper will be listed as Sichuan or black, and should be freshly ground if possible.

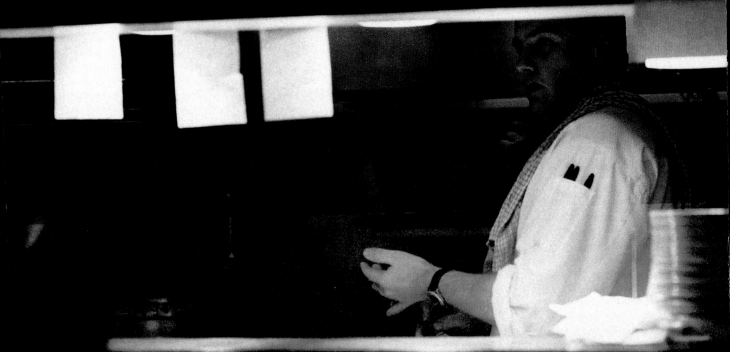

basics

brown chicken stock

3 kg (6 lb) chicken
carcasses

2 teaspoons olive oil

2 large carrots, sliced

1 large brown
onion, sliced

½ head celery, sliced

5 cloves garlic, sliced

1 teaspoon black
peppercorns

I prefer to use this richer stock, rather than the usual white chicken stock. Roasting the chicken carcasses gives the stock a deep reddish-brown colour and a fuller flavour.

Preheat the oven to 220ºC (425ºF). Wash the carcasses to remove any blood and lingering scraps of innards. Roast the chicken carcasses for about 30 minutes, turning constantly, until they are dark brown.

Meanwhile, heat the olive oil in a large 5 litre (10 pint) stockpot and sauté the carrots, onion, celery, garlic and peppercorns until golden brown. Stir constantly to stop the vegetables burning.

Add the roasted bones to the stockpot and cover with cold water. Bring to the boil then lower the heat and simmer gently for 5–6 hours. From time to time you will need to skim away any scum and fat that rises to the surface. Top up with a little extra water as you skim. Strain the stock through a fine sieve into another large clean pot and allow it to cool. Skim off any fat that rises as it cools. Return the stock to the boil and simmer until the stock is reduced by half, skimming frequently. Pour into a clean container and allow to cool completely before refrigerating or freezing.

Makes 2 litres (4 pints)

asian-style duck stock

2 kg (4 lb)
duck carcasses,
roughly chopped

2 tablespoons
olive oil

1 carrot, sliced

1 brown onion, sliced

½ head celery, sliced

100 ml (3½ fl oz)
Shao Xing wine
(Chinese cooking wine)

30 ml (1 fl oz)
light soy sauce

1 tablespoon
Sichuan peppercorns

½ bunch
coriander (cilantro)

3 litres (6 pints) water

I use this Asian-style duck stock as a base for many poultry dishes – particularly for those with an Asian influence.

Preheat the oven to 200ºC (400ºF). Roast the duck carcasses for about an hour, turning occasionally, until they are dark brown.

Meanwhile, heat the olive oil in a large 5 litre (10 pint) stockpot and sauté the carrots, onion and celery until golden brown. Stir constantly to stop the vegetables burning.

Rest the roasted duck carcasses on absorbent paper then add them to the stockpot with the cooking wine, soy sauce, peppercorns and coriander. Cover with cold water and bring to the boil, then lower the heat and simmer very gently for at least 4 hours. Be careful not to let the stock boil, or it will become cloudy. From time to time you will need to skim away any scum and fat that rises to the surface. Top up with a little extra water as you skim. Strain the stock into another large clean pot and allow it to cool. Skim off any fat that rises as it cools. Return the stock to the boil and simmer until it is reduced by a third, skimming frequently. Pour into a clean container and allow to cool completely before refrigerating or freezing.

Makes 2 litres (4 pints)

veal stock

3 kg (6 lb) veal
neck bones

2 teaspoons
olive oil

2 carrots, sliced

1 large brown
onion, sliced

½ head
celery, sliced

5 cloves garlic

1 sprig thyme

1 bay leaf

1 teaspoon black
peppercorns

250 ml (9 fl oz) red wine

This is the base stock that I use for most meat dishes in this book.

Preheat the oven to 220°C (425°F). Roast the veal bones for about an hour, until they are dark brown.

Meanwhile, heat the olive oil in a large 5 litre (10 pint) stockpot and sauté the carrots, onion, celery, garlic, herbs and peppercorns until golden brown. Stir constantly to stop the vegetables burning. Add the red wine and simmer until reduced by half.

Add the roasted bones to the stockpot and cover with cold water. Bring to the boil then lower the heat and simmer gently for 6 hours. From time to time you will need to skim away any scum and fat that rises to the surface. Strain the stock through a fine sieve into another large clean pot and allow it to cool. Skim off any fat that rises as it cools. Return the stock to the boil and simmer until the stock is reduced by half, skimming frequently. Pour into a clean container and allow to cool completely before refrigerating or freezing.

Makes 2 litres (4 pints)

master stock

3 litres (6 pints) water

250 ml (9 fl oz) light
soy sauce

500 ml (16 fl oz)
Shao Xing wine
(Chinese cooking wine)

200 g (7 oz) yellow
rock sugar

40 g (1½ oz) fresh ginger

5 cloves garlic

3 cardamom pods

2 cinnamon sticks

10 g (2 teaspoons)
dried mandarin peel

Spices for Bag

4 whole cloves

4 star anise

1 teaspoon sichuan pepper

1 teaspoon licorice root

1 teaspoon dried chilli

1 teaspoon cumin seeds

1 teaspoon fennel seeds

This Asian master stock is a key ingredient in my kitchen. Master stocks are essential for the red-braised dishes of China. The soy sauce gives a rich reddish-brown colour to any meat or poultry, while the Chinese wine, rock sugar and spices impart a unique flavour.

The master stock can be used over and over again and it will grow better and richer over time. However it is important to follow a few essential rules to prevent harmful bacteria growing. Only ever use a master stock to cook one type of meat – i.e. only chicken, or duck or pork. It is not a multi-purpose stock. After each use, bring the stock back to the boil, and then skim it and strain through a fine sieve into a clean sealable container. Allow it to cool completely before refrigerating or freezing.

Place all of the spices into a piece of muslin cloth and tie into a bag. Put the spice bag along with all of the other ingredients in a large stockpot and bring to the boil. Simmer gently for 10–15 minutes to allow the spices to infuse. Allow the stock to cool completely before pouring into a clean container. Leave the aromatics in the stock overnight to intensify the flavours. Refrigerate or freeze until needed.

Makes 4 litres (8 pints)

beer batter

500 g (1 lb) self-raising flour

pinch of salt

1 teaspoon olive oil

500 ml (16 fl oz) beer

This produces a lovely crisp batter and is particularly good for frying vegetables and delicate white fish such as whiting and garfish. I use it for frying Zucchini Flower Fritters (see page 47).

Sieve the flour into a large basin and add the salt and olive oil. Pour in about one third of the beer and whisk to a smooth paste. Make sure there are no lumps (use your fingers to break them down), and gradually whisk in the remaining beer. Leave the batter to stand for 20 minutes before use.

Makes 700 ml (22 fl oz)

tempura batter

100 g (3½ oz)
cornflour (cornstarch)

75 g (3 oz) plain
(all-purpose) flour

pinch of salt

100 ml (3½ fl oz)
chilled lime juice

100 ml (3½ fl oz)
chilled lemon juice

A batter used for deep-frying in the Japanese style. Tempura batter is particularly good for deep-frying thinly sliced vegetables, seafood and poultry. At its best, it provides a thin, almost translucent crispy coating, and should never be gluggy. I use if for Tempura Fried Quail (see page 62).

Sieve the flours and salt into a mixing bowl. Whisk in the lime and lemon juices. The batter should be smooth and lump-free. Keep refrigerated and use within 2 hours.

Makes 300 ml (10 fl oz)

tamarind paste

150 g (5 oz) seedless
tamarind pulp

75 ml (3 fl oz) warm water

Tamarind paste and tamarind water are used in many Asian dishes to add a distinctive fruity-sour flavour. I use tamarind paste to achieve a really strong dominant sour flavour in more robust dishes. Tamarind water works well in soups and broths when a lighter flavour is required.

Mix the tamarind pulp and water in a bowl. Squeeze with your hands to loosen the pulp and rub with your fingers to make a paste. Push through a sieve to remove any remaining seeds. Store in a non-reactive container in the refrigerator, where it will keep for several days.

Makes around 100 g (3½ oz)

tamarind water

100 g (3½ oz)
seedless tamarind pulp

350 ml (12 fl oz) warm water

To make tamarind water, mix the tamarind pulp and water in a bowl. Use your hands to squeeze the pulp and help it dissolve. Strain the liquid through a sieve and discard the fibre and any seeds. Store in a non-reactive container in the refrigerator, where it will keep for several days.

Makes about 400 ml (13 fl oz)

sticky soy

200 ml (7 fl oz)
light soy sauce

200 ml (7 fl oz) sweet soy
sauce (ketjap manis)

100 ml (3½ oz) honey

I love to use sticky soy in all sorts of dishes. Not only does it look very dramatic swirled on plain white plates, but the sweet-saltiness perfectly complements the heat of wasabi, chilli and pickled ginger. I particularly like to use sticky soy with Tuna Sashimi and Wonton Stack (see page 53) Lime-Cured Cuttlefish (see page 49), and Crispy Duck and Wonton Stack (see page117).

My preferred light soy sauce is a Taiwanese brand, and my preferred ketjap manis is Indonesian. Both these are readily available in Asian supermarkets.

Place all the ingredients in a saucepan and simmer gently until reduced by two-thirds. When cool the sticky soy should be the consistency of honey. (Test the consistency on a cold plate while the syrup is cooking.) Pour into an airtight container and store in a cool dark place where it will keep for up to 2 weeks.

Makes 200 ml (7 fl oz)

sugar syrup

250 g (9 oz) caster
(superfine) sugar

250 ml (9 fl oz) water

Place all ingredients in a non-reactive saucepan and bring to the boil and turn off.

Makes 600 ml (20 fl oz)

balsamic syrup

200 ml (7 fl oz)
balsamic vinegar

175 g (6 oz) white sugar

50 ml (1½ fl oz) water

Balsamic vinegar adds a lovely sour dimension to a classic sweet sugar syrup and works really well in a lot of my dishes. I particularly like it with certain cheeses – I use it for the Whitelaw Cheese Salad with Fresh Figs (see page 74) and for Grilled Swordfish with Baked Eggplant, Whipped Mascarpone and Goat's Cheese (see page 103). It is also delicious drizzled over strawberries. Naturally, the better quality vinegar you use, the better the syrup will be.

Put the vinegar, sugar and water into a non-reactive saucepan and bring to the boil. Simmer until the syrup is reduced by a half to two-thirds. To test the consistency of the syrup while cooking, drop a teaspoonful onto a plate. When cool it should have the consistency of honey.

Pour the hot syrup into a sterilised jar and seal. Store in a cool place where it will keep for up to 2 weeks.

Makes 200 ml (7 fl oz)

gula melaka syrup

300 g (10½ oz) dark palm sugar, roughly chopped

150 ml (5 fl oz) water

10 g (2 teaspoons) dried mandarin peel or the peel of 1 fresh mandarin, roughly chopped

1 cinnamon stick, roughly chopped

A key ingredient to have on hand, as I use this syrup in many of my recipes. It is the third member of the trio (with lime juice and fish sauce) used as a seasoning in many South East Asian dishes. The deep rich flavour of the palm sugar works well in balancing sour and salty flavours and in tempering the heat of many chilli-hot dishes.

Place all the ingredients in a non-reactive saucepan and bring to the boil. Lower the heat and simmer until the syrup is reduced by about one third, and is the consistency of runny honey. From time to time you may need to skim away any scum that rises to the surface. Remove from the heat and pour the syrup into a clean container (leave the mandarin peel and cinnamon in the syrup so the flavours intensify). Once cool, refrigerate until ready to serve. Gula melaka syrup keeps for around 2 weeks in a sealed jar in the refrigerator.

Makes 250 ml (9 fl oz)

candied chillies

10 red Lombok chillies

150 g (5 oz) white sugar

100 ml (3½ fl oz) Japanese
rice wine vinegar

100 ml (3½ fl oz) water

Simmering long red chillies in sugar syrup really brings out the sweetness of their natural sugars. I often use candied chillies in salads, such as the Avocado, Mango and Pink Grapefruit Salad (see page 93) where the sweetness and heat work really well with the buttery richness of avocado and the sweetness of the mango. Candied Chillies are also a great match with soy and sesame flavours.

Wash the chillies well, then slice crosswise into thin rings. Put into a bowl of cold water and wash out the inner seeds. Drain well and dry in a salad spinner – this also helps get rid of any remaining seeds

Place the sugar, vinegar and water in a wide, medium-size pan and bring to a gentle simmer. Reduce by two-thirds, brushing down the inside of the pan with water from time to time to stop it crystallising. Just before the syrup begins to caramelise, add the chillies and simmer for 10 minutes, or until the chillies are tender. Remove from the heat, allow to cool and refrigerate until needed. It is best to use the candied chillies within a week or so, as they do sometimes crystallise once refrigerated.

Makes 500 ml (16 fl oz)

peanut praline

200 g (7 oz) roasted
unsalted peanuts

200 ml (7 fl oz) water

250 g (9 oz) caster
(superfine) sugar

Preheat the oven to 160°C (325°F). Spread the peanuts out onto a small baking sheet and roast for about 10 minutes, or until golden brown. Tip them onto another flat tray lined with baking paper or lightly greased kitchen foil.

Put the sugar and water into a saucepan and bring to the boil. Lower the heat and simmer for about 10 minutes, or until the syrup caramelises. From time to time you will need to brush the insides of the pan with water to stop it crystallising.

Pour the caramel onto the roasted peanuts and let harden. Break into small pieces and store in a sealed container in the freezer.

Makes 300 g (10 oz)

toasted coconut milk

1 whole coconut

This is a technique that I learnt in Bali. It extracts the maximum amount of flavour from the coconut and the distinctive nutty liquid can be used in all kinds of recipes. I particularly like to use it in ice-creams and sorbets, such as Coconut, Chilli and Lime Sorbet (see page 163) and in other desserts. It also works well in some savoury dishes and in soup bases. The remaining coconut flesh can also be used, for instance in Green Coconut Pancakes (page 163).

When purchasing coconuts choose heavy ones. Also choose from suppliers with a large turnover. Coconuts often go sour very quickly, and this cannot always be detected. One way to detect sourness is if upon shaking you hear water.

Use a hammer to crack the coconut open and discard the water inside. Use a small sharp knife or screwdriver to prise the coconut flesh away from the hard outer shell – there will still be a layer of dark skin attached. (If you find it difficult to work the flesh away from the outer shell, warm the coconut in the oven for a few minutes.) Cut the coconut into pieces and place on a naked flame, skin side down. Toast the coconut until the skin nearly blackens – this is how you achieve the correct nutty toasted flavour.

Allow to cool, then grate the coconut, dark skin included, very finely. This is the key part of the process, as the coconut flesh must be grated almost to a powder to release all the natural oils and flavour. If you can, use a special coconut grater (I use a Balinese one), or a very fine grater available from specialty food equipment suppliers.

Once the coconut has been grated, put it into a large bowl and add the same quantity of warm water. Allow to stand for a few minutes while the coconut absorbs the water. Use your hands to squeeze the coconut mixture to extract as much flavour as possible. Strain the water and store in the refrigerator where it will keep for several days.

1 coconut should yield around 2 cups coconut milk and 2 cups coconut flesh

egg wash

100 ml (3½ fl oz) milk
3 eggs

Egg wash is an integral part of the crumbing process for many deep-fried dishes. I also use it for sealing hand-made pasta.

Put the milk and eggs in a bowl and whisk until well combined. Use within 24 hours.

Makes 250 ml (9 fl oz)

prickly ash

3 tablespoons sea salt

1 tablespoon whole
Sichuan peppercorns

So called because the pepper really does prickle the tongue. It's an essential seasoning in many Asian dishes, and is often sprinkled on roasted meats and poultry (it is too harsh for most seafood). At ezard we serve it with parmesan-infused olive oil as an aromatic accompaniment to bread at the start of the meal. It really wakes up the palate.

Dry-roast the sea salt and peppercorns in a wok or frying-pan over a gentle heat until fragrant, about 2–3 minutes. Shake the pan frequently so the mix doesn't burn. Allow to cool then use a mortar and pestle to grind to a fine powder. Pass through a fine sieve to remove any husks. Store in a sealed container in a dry place. Prickly ash is at its best used within 7 days, as the pepper loses its fragrance quite quickly once cooked and ground.

Makes 4 tablespoons

wafer mix

150 g (5 oz) softened
unsalted butter

250 g (9 oz) icing
(confectioners')
sugar, sifted

3 egg whites

1 whole egg

200 g (7 oz)
plain (all-purpose)
flour, sifted

I use these buttery wafer biscuits as a garnish for many desserts – particularly ice-creams and sorbets, such as Blood Orange and Aperol Sorbet Stack (see page 139) and Pink Grapefruit, Coriander and Gin Sorbet (see page 142).

Cream the butter and the sugar until pale. In a separate bowl, whisk together the egg whites and whole egg. Stir the eggs into the creamed butter and sugar, and then sift over the flour. Mix briefly until incorporated. Refrigerate for at least 30 minutes before use, but the mix will keep well for up to 3 or 4 days.

Makes 600 g (1¼ lb)

roasted rice

100 g (3½ oz)
jasmine rice

15 g (½ oz) sea salt

A very versatile condiment to have in the kitchen. I use roasted rice as a garnish for many Asian salads, such as Tea-Smoked Duck Salad with Cucumber, Chilli and Lime (see page 67) and Hot and Sour Thai Beef Salad (see page 72). It also makes a deliciously nutty crusting on fried fish, for example Baby Snapper with Roasted Rice Crust (see page 84).

Preheat the oven to 200ºC (400ºF). Spread the rice out on a small baking tray and roast until golden brown, about 15 minutes. You will need to shake the tray every few minutes so the rice browns evenly. Allow the rice to cool completely. Place the roasted rice in a mortar with the salt, or use a spice grinder, and grind to a very fine powder. Sieve through a fine strainer and store in a sealed container in a dry place. The finer you grind the rice, the better the result.

Makes 100 g (3½ oz)

jasmine rice

420 g (14½ oz)
jasmine rice

500 ml (1 pint)
water

Jasmine rice is also known as Thai fragrant rice, and is the variety I like to use best as an accompaniment to my dishes. It is long-grained and wonderfully aromatic.

When it comes to cooking jasmine rice I prefer to use an electric rice cooker (see section on cooking equipment) as it is very easy and always produces a good result.

If you don't have an electric rice cooker, then use the absorption method that works best for you. Remember that the most important thing is to get the rice-to-water ratio correct, although this will differ depending on the type of rice you are cooking. For a long-grained rice such as jasmine, you will need around 1½ cups of water to 1 cup of rice. To serve six people generously, use about 3 cups of rice and 4½ cups water.

However you plan to cook it, first place the rice in a colander and wash it under cold running water until the water runs clear. This is an important step a it washes away excess starch. Drain the rice well then tip it into an electric rice cooker. Add the water and cook according to the manufacturer's instructions. Alternatively, cook according to the absorption method you prefer.

Do not add salt to the rice as it cooks as it spoils the delicate flavour of jasmine rice.

Serves 6

crispy shallot garnish

5 cloves garlic

4 red shallots

20 g (¾ oz) fresh ginger

2 red Lombok chillies

500 ml (16 fl oz) peanut oil

salt

caster (superfine) sugar

This is the classic garnish I use in many dishes to provide textural interest. I like to season crispy garnishes with sugar and salt to add another flavour dimension.

Peel the garlic, shallots and ginger. Use a Japanese binriner (slicer) or a very sharp knife to slice them wafer-thin. Slice the chillies very finely on an angle.

Heat the peanut oil to 160ºC (325ºF) in a wok or a deep-fryer. Fry each ingredient separately until golden brown. They should float freely in the bubbling oil as they cook. Remove from the oil as they brown with a slotted spoon and allow to drain on absorbent paper. Season lightly to taste with salt and sugar.

Note: A binriner is a Japanese hand slicer. It is made from hard plastic and is easy to clean. It comes with a hand-guard for cautious cooks. Binriners are readily available from Asian stores and catering equipment stores.

Makes about 1 cup

pickled green papaya

1 green papaya

200 ml (7 fl oz) water

200 ml (7 fl oz) rice wine vinegar

200 g (7 oz) white sugar

1 red bird's eye chilli

This is often added to Thai salads with peanuts, beans and chillies – it is fairly pungent so is not usually eaten on its own. I use it in the Tempura Fried Quail with Green Papaya, Pomelo and Peanut Salad (see page 62) and in Coconut Fried Garfish With Vietnamese Rice Noodle Salad (page 91).

Peel the papaya, cut it in half and scoop out the seeds. Cut the flesh into julienne strips and place in a large airtight container.

Put the water, vinegar, sugar and chilli into a small non-reactive saucepan and bring to the boil, making sure the sugar dissolves completely. Pour the boiling liquid onto the papaya and allow to cool. Seal the container and store in the fridge for 4 weeks before using.

Makes 300 g (10½ oz)

pickled ginger

300 g (10½ oz) fresh
ginger, peeled

200 ml (7 fl oz) water

200 ml (7 fl oz) rice
wine vinegar

200 g (7 oz) caster
(superfine) sugar

1 red bird's eye chilli

A popular accompaniment to Japanese dishes, in particular sushi and sashimi.

I think its refreshingly light flavour complements all kinds of seafood dishes, such as Steamed Crab Wontons with Avocado, Tomato, Lime and Black Olive Salad (see page 33), Japanese-Inspired Oyster Shooters (see page 44) and Tuna Sashimi and Wonton Stack (see page 53). If possible, try to find really young stem ginger.

Peel ginger then bring a saucepan of cold water to the boil and blanch the ginger for 20 seconds, then refresh in cold water. Repeat 5 times to extract any bitterness from the ginger and to soften the flesh. Transfer the ginger to a large airtight container.

In another small non-reactive saucepan mix together the 200 ml (7 fl oz) water with the vinegar, sugar and chilli. Bring to the boil making sure the sugar dissolves completely. Pour the boiling liquid onto the ginger and allow to cool. Seal the container and store in the fridge for 4 weeks.

To use pickled ginger in a dish, remove it from the liquid and cut into fine dice or julienne strips according to the dish. Pickled ginger juice may need to be slightly diluted, as it is fairly pungent.

Makes 300 g (10½ oz) pickled ginger and 500 ml (16 fl oz) ginger juice

pickled bean shoots

150 ml (5 fl oz) mirin

150 ml (5 fl oz) rice
wine vinegar

75 ml (3 fl oz) light
soy sauce

1 tablespoon grated
palm sugar

50 g (2 oz) fresh
bean shoots

These are a lovely crunchy addition to Thai salads.

Put the mirin, vinegar, soy sauce and palm sugar into a non-reactive bowl and whisk together until the sugar has completely dissolved. Add the bean shoots and marinate in the refrigerator for 30 minutes before using. Use them within 2 hours so they retain their lovely crunchiness.

Makes 50 g (2 oz)

fish (blue eye) mousse

150 g (5 oz) white fish

1 egg white

110 ml (4 fl oz)
pure cream

sea salt

I use this fish mousse as a binding agent in seafood pasta and dumplings. I prefer to use blue eye, however, if this is not available, use a sweet white fish such as whiting or sole.

Trim the fish of its fins, skin and any blood. Dice the flesh and put into a food processor. Blend to a smooth purée and, with the motor running, add the egg white. Pass through a fine sieve into a clean, chilled bowl and stir in the cream with a wooden spoon. Season to taste and refrigerate. Use within 24 hours.

Makes 250 g (9 oz)

chicken mousse

220 g (8 oz)
chicken breast

1 egg white

100 ml (3½ fl oz)
thickened cream

sea salt

freshly ground
black pepper

I use this chicken mousse as a binding agent in pasta and dumplings that have a meat or poultry filling. I prefer to use free-range organic chicken as the flesh has a distinctively sweet flavour.

Trim away any visible skin, blood or sinews from the chicken breast and slice into small pieces. Put the chicken into a food processor with the egg white and blend to a smooth purée. Pass the purée through a fine sieve to remove any sinews that have not broken down. Weigh out 200 g (7 oz) and place in a chilled bowl. Use a wooden spoon to mix in the cream. Season to taste and refrigerate. Use within 24 hours.

Makes 300 g (10 oz)

basic pasta dough

340 g (12 oz) strong
plain (all-purpose) flour

2 eggs

2 egg yolks

2 tablespoons water

2 tablespoons olive oil

extra flour for dusting

Sift the flour into a mixing bowl and make a well in the centre. In a separate bowl whisk together the eggs, egg yolks and water. Pour the egg mixture into the flour with the olive oil and combine with your fingers to make a dough. Tip onto a floured work surface and knead well until the dough becomes smooth and elastic, about 3–5 minutes. Wrap in plastic wrap and allow it to rest in the refrigerator for at least 25 minutes.

Remove the dough from the fridge and divide into two flattish rectangles, about 8 cm (3½ in) wide. Set the rollers on a pasta machine to the widest setting and run each piece of dough through 3 times. Fold each piece in half and run through the widest setting another 5 times. Reduce the rollers to the next widest setting and run each piece of dough through twice. Continue in this way, running each piece of dough through each setting twice, finishing with the thinnest. Make sure you keep the work surface well-dusted with flour as you work. Use as soon as possible, and keep the dough covered with a damp cloth as you work.

Makes 500 g (1 lb)

mashed potato

600 g (1¼ lb)
unpeeled potatoes

100 g (3½ oz)
unsalted butter

100 ml (3½ fl oz)
thickened cream

50 ml (1½ fl oz)
extra-virgin olive oil

1 teaspoon grated
parmesan cheese

salt

ground black
pepper (optional)

Put the potatoes in a medium-size saucepan and cover with cold water. Bring to the boil, then lower the heat and simmer gently until tender. Tip the potatoes into a colander and let them sit and steam-dry for a few minutes as they drain. Peel the potatoes and push them through a fine sieve or potato ricer. Return to the saucepan, add the butter, cream, olive oil and parmesan cheese and heat very gently until the butter has melted and the potatoes are smooth and creamy. Season to taste and serve straight away.

Serves 6

artichokes

6 globe artichokes

1.5 litres
(2½ pints) water

50 ml (1½ fl oz)
olive oil

5 cloves garlic,
peeled and bruised

2 teaspoons
fresh rosemary

1 lemon

1 teaspoon
sea salt

Cut the stem off each artichoke, leaving about 5 cm (1½ in) attached. Trim off the top quarter of each artichoke and snap away the hard outer leaves. Using a vegetable peeler, shave away the rough outer layer of the stalk and artichoke base.

Place the remaining ingredients in a medium-size non-reactive pan and bring to the boil. Drop the artichokes into the boiling liquid, then lower the heat and simmer gently for around 20 minutes. You may need to cover the artichokes with a plate to keep them submerged. Test the artichokes with a skewer or toothpick to see if they are tender.

When the artichokes are cooked, remove from the heat and allow them to cool in the stock. Transfer to a container and refrigerate in the stock until ready to use. The artichokes will keep for 2–3 days.

Note: To clean the artichoke once cooked, remove from the stock and peel outer leaves, cut the artichoke in half and, using a small knife or teaspoon, scrape out the furry 'choke' from the inner part of the artichoke, as it is too bitter to eat.

Makes 6

labna yoghurt cheese

1 kg (2 lb)
plain yoghurt

Rinse a 30 x 30 cm (12 x 12 in) square of muslin under cold water then squeeze dry. While the cloth is still damp, spoon the yoghurt into the centre of the cloth, bring the 4 corners together and tie with string. Very gently squeeze any excess water from the yoghurt then suspend over a deep bowl and put in the refrigerator to drain for 24–48 hours. The longer the hanging time, the firmer the resulting cheese will be. Remove the cheese from the muslin and store in an airtight container in the refrigerator.

Makes 600 g (1¼ lb)

starters

jerusalem artichoke soup
with chestnut and vanilla cream

Jerusalem Artichoke Soup

1.5 kg (3 lb)
Jerusalem artichokes

juice of 1 lemon

salt

50 g (2 oz)
unsalted butter

1 medium leek,
white part only,
finely sliced

3 cloves garlic,
finely sliced

4 shallots, finely sliced

1 litre (1¾ pints)
brown chicken stock
(see Basics)

salt and black pepper

Chestnut and Vanilla Cream

500 ml (16 fl oz)
vegetable oil

125 g (4½ oz) fresh
chestnuts, peeled

1 vanilla bean, split

200 ml (7 fl oz) milk

50 ml (2 fl oz)
thickened cream

Garnish

6 sprigs chervil

1 teaspoon freshly
ground black pepper

For me, this is the ultimate winter soup, with the earthy, almost basic flavours of the Jerusalem artichoke enlivened by the sweet spiciness of vanilla. I think it's a good example of how experimenting with flavours can be so rewarding; often the most unusual combinations really do work well together.

Soup: Peel the artichokes, slice them thinly and rub all over with the lemon juice and salt. Place the artichokes in a colander for 1–2 hours, so that any bitter juices may drain away. Rinse them well then pat dry.

Melt the butter in a medium-size saucepan, then add the leek, garlic and shallots. Sweat for 5–10 minutes, stirring from time to time, until they soften, but do not colour. Add the artichokes, stir well and sweat for 2–3 more minutes. Pour in the chicken stock, season with salt and pepper and simmer for 15 minutes, or until the artichokes are tender. Remove from the heat and allow to cool slightly. Purée in batches in a food processor, then pass through a strainer into a clean saucepan.

Chestnut and Vanilla Cream: In a small pan heat the vegetable oil to 180ºC (350ºF). Add the peeled chestnuts, a few at a time, and 'blanch' for 1–2 minutes, or until the skin starts to lift away. Remove from the oil and drain on absorbent paper. When cool enough to handle, peel away the skin with your fingers (or rub them vigorously in a towel).

Place the chestnuts in a small heavy-based, non-reactive saucepan with the vanilla bean and milk. Simmer gently for an hour, or until the chestnuts are tender. Remove the vanilla bean, scrape out the seeds and add them to the cooked chestnuts. Purée in a food processor, then pass through a fine sieve. Stir in the cream and combine well.

To Serve: Reheat the soup until simmering gently, taste and adjust seasoning if necessary. Ladle into soup bowls and top with a spoonful of the chestnut and vanilla cream. Garnish with a sprig of chervil and a sprinkle of freshly ground black pepper.

Serves 6

middle eastern-spiced red bean soup

Spice Mix

½ teaspoon sumac

½ teaspoon paprika

½ teaspoon ground cumin

½ teaspoon black pepper

½ teaspoon ground cloves

¼ teaspoon fenugreek

¼ teaspoon
ground cinnamon

Soup

100 g (3½ oz) adzuki beans (soaked in water overnight)

1 small onion, peeled and cut into quarters

1 teaspoon olive oil

500 g (1 lb) lamb strap cut into small cubes

1 medium onion, finely diced

1.5 litres
(2½ pints) water

4 cloves garlic, finely chopped

1 bay leaf

3 red bird's eye chillies, finely chopped

1 teaspoon sea salt

2 potatoes, peeled and cut into 1 cm (½ in) dice

3 carrots, peeled and cut into 1 cm (½ in)

2 red capsicums (bell peppers), roasted, peeled and diced

1 tablespoon red wine vinegar

salt and black pepper

Garnish

½ cup labna (see Basics)

1 teaspoon fresh dill

1 teaspoon fresh coriander (cilantro) leaves

1 teaspoon fresh parsley

1 teaspoon fresh oregano

Spice Mix: Prepare the spice mix by combining all the ingredients thoroughly.

Soup: Drain the adzuki beans of their soaking liquid, rinse them well and tip into a medium-size pot. Add the onion quarters, cover with fresh water and bring to the boil. Cook until the beans are tender, about 45 minutes. You will need to top up the water from time to time. Once the beans are cooked, strain off the liquid and remove and discard the onion.

In a clean pot, heat the olive oil, add the lamb strap and sauté until golden brown all over. Add the finely diced onion and sauté for a further 5 minutes, until golden brown. Now cover with 1½ litres of water and bring to a gentle simmer. Add the garlic, bay leaves, chillies and sea salt and simmer until the lamb is tender, about 15–20 minutes. Next, add the diced potatoes, carrots and capsicum to the soup with the cooked adzuki beans. Add the prepared spice mix, stir well and simmer for 20–30 minutes. Add the vinegar and season to taste with salt and pepper.

To Serve: When ready to serve, bring the soup back to a gentle simmer, taste and adjust seasoning if necessary. Ladle into soup bowls, top with a blob of labna and a generous amount of fresh herb garnish.

Serves 6

soup pastes

Wet spice pastes form the basis for many South East Asian dishes, and I use them constantly in my cooking, in everything from light broths to richer laksas and curries and in accompanying condiments such as sambals and relishes.

Wet pastes use a blend of fresh ingredients such as garlic, ginger, coriander (cilantro) root, galangal, turmeric, lemongrass and chilli. Traditionally these ingredients are ground by hand using a mortar and pestle to extract the maximum flavour. They are then blended to taste to give each dish its own character and complexity.

As is usually the case in cuisines that depend upon an oral tradition, there is rarely a right or wrong when it comes to the proportions of various ingredients used in spice blends and pastes. While there is a general aim to achieve a balance between hot, sour, salty and sweet, each cook will have his or her own preference and taste for achieving that balance.

Because they use fresh ingredients, wet spice blends don't have a long lifespan and should be used quickly for the maximum flavour impact, but it is this freshness that gives a dish its purity of flavour and vitality.

hot and sour chicken soup

Soup Paste

1 teaspoon
shrimp paste

40 g (1½ oz) fresh
ginger, peeled and
finely chopped

40 g (1½ oz) fresh
galangal, peeled and
finely chopped

3 cloves garlic, peeled
and finely chopped

2 tablespoons fresh
turmeric, peeled and
finely chopped

1 lemongrass stalk,
white part only,
finely chopped

4 fresh or frozen
kaffir lime leaves

3 red bird's eye chillies

¼ cup coriander
(cilantro) leaves

Soup

300 g (10 oz) chicken
breasts, skin removed

30 ml (1 fl oz) peanut oil

1.5 litres (2½ pints)
brown chicken stock
(see Basics)

½ cup seedless
tamarind paste

200 g (7 oz) fresh
egg noodles

50 g (2 oz) palm sugar

50 ml (2 fl oz) fish sauce

50 ml (2 fl oz) lime juice

Garnish

20 g (¾ oz) fresh
ginger, peeled and
very thinly sliced

1 long red chilli, finely
sliced lengthwise

5 spring onions
(scallions), white part
only, very thinly sliced

½ lemongrass stalk,
white part only, very
thinly sliced

¼ cup coriander
(cilantro) leaves, plus a
few extra for decoration

50 g (2 oz) snow
peas, finely sliced
on the diagonal

Soup Paste: Preheat the oven to 180ºC (350ºF). Wrap the shrimp paste in a piece of kitchen foil and roast until fragrant (about 4–6 minutes).

Place the ginger, galangal, garlic, turmeric, lemongrass, lime leaves, chillies and coriander leaves in a food processor, or use a mortar and pestle, and grind to a fine paste. Stir in the shrimp paste.

Soup: Slice the chicken fillets into bite-size strips. Heat the peanut oil in a medium frying pan, then add the chicken pieces and sauté, a few at a time, until golden brown. Remove from the oil and drain on absorbent paper. Reserve until ready to serve.

Add the soup paste to the frying pan and cook until fragrant, about 15 minutes. Stir frequently to ensure the paste doesn't burn. Transfer the soup paste to a large non-reactive saucepan, add the chicken stock and tamarind paste and bring to the boil. Lower the heat and allow to simmer gently for a further 20 minutes. From time to time you will need to skim off any scum that floats to the top. Strain through a fine sieve and reserve until ready to serve.

Garnish: Mix together the finely sliced ginger, chilli, spring onions, lemongrass, coriander leaves and snow peas and refrigerate until needed.

To Serve: Bring the soup back to a simmer. Add the egg noodles and the chicken pieces. Season the soup with the palm sugar, fish sauce and lime juice, adjusting the balance until you get a nice balance of hot, salty and sour. Divide the garnish, egg noodles and chicken pieces between six large soup bowls. Pour over the soup and finish with a few coriander leaves. Serve straight away.

Serves 6

spicy prawn wontons
in coconut and coriander soup

Soup Paste

1 tablespoon
shrimp paste

1 teaspoon
coriander seeds

6 red shallots, peeled
and roughly chopped

3 cloves garlic,
roughly chopped

40 g (1½ oz) fresh
galangal, peeled and
roughly chopped

40 g (1½ oz) fresh
ginger, peeled and
roughly chopped

1 lemongrass stalk,
white part only,
roughly chopped

2 long red chillies,
roughly chopped

1 red bird's eye chilli,
roughly chopped

2 fresh or frozen
kaffir lime leaves,
roughly chopped

25 g (1 oz) candlenuts
(about 8)

4 coriander (cilantro)
roots, roughly chopped

Coconut and Coriander Soup

1.5 litres (2½ pints)
coconut milk

60 ml (2 fl oz) lime juice

50 ml (1½ fl oz)
fish sauce

30 ml (1 fl oz) gula melaka
syrup (see Basics)

Spicy Prawn Wontons

200 g (7 oz) whole
green prawns (reserve
the shell and head
for the prawn oil)

1 red bird's eye chilli,
finely chopped

2 coriander (cilantro)
roots, finely chopped

1 medium spring onion
(scallion), finely chopped

1 teaspoon light
soy sauce

½ teaspoon
sesame oil

36 wonton skins,
at room temperature

Spicy Prawn Oil

prawn shells and heads

100 ml (3½ fl oz)
pure olive oil

1 teaspoon tomato paste

½ red bird's eye chilli

Garnish

¼ cup coriander
(cilantro) leaves

¼ cup Vietnamese mint

2 tablespoons crispy
shallots (see Basics)

To call a laksa (which is what this dish really is) simply a soup is to completely under-sell it! Laksas really are fantastic dishes and this one is a real winner. The creamy coconut base is intensely fragrant with myriad flavour sensations. Because it is so rich and filling, it makes sense to serve it in a small cup (what the French call a 'demi tasse') or in a small Chinese rice bowl. If you find it too irresistible, team it with a smaller main course, or head straight to a fruit-based dessert.

Soup Paste: Preheat the oven to 180°C (350°F). Wrap the shrimp paste in a piece of kitchen foil and roast until fragrant (about 4–6 minutes). Lightly roast the coriander seeds in a dry pan. Put them in a food processor with the remaining ingredients. Blitz until smooth then stir in the roasted shrimp paste.

Coconut and Coriander Soup: In a medium saucepan, heat 250 ml (9 fl oz) of the coconut milk until it splits (you will know when this happens: the coconut solids fall to the bottom of the pot and the oil floats on the top). Add the soup paste, mix well and cook for 15–20 minutes. Stir frequently to ensure it doesn't burn. Add the rest of the coconut milk and bring back to a gentle simmer. Cook for 15–20 minutes, until the soup is fragrant, taking care not to let it boil. Strain through a fine sieve and reserve.

Spicy Prawn Wontons: Peel the prawns and remove the heads and tails. Reserve the prawn shells and heads for making the prawn oil. With a sharp knife, split each prawn along the back and carefully ease away the intestines. Finely chop the prawn meat and place in a mixing bowl with the finely chopped chilli, coriander and spring onion. Add the soy sauce and sesame oil and mix well.

Lay 18 wonton wrappers onto a dry flat surface and place ½ teaspoon of the prawn mixture in the centre of each one. Lightly brush around the edges of each wonton skin with water then top with the remaining 18 wonton skins. Use your fingers to press the edges together and seal the dumplings well. Use a small 4 cm (1½ in) cookie-cutter to cut each dumpling into a neat circle. Refrigerate on a plastic wrap-lined tray until ready to cook

Spicy Prawn Oil: Wash the prawn heads and shells and dry them thoroughly, inside and out. It is essential that they are totally dry, or the resulting oil will be cloudy. You may prefer to dry them in a low oven for 5–10 minutes

Heat the olive oil in a small saucepan. Add the prawn heads and shells and fry over a medium flame until fragrant, about 2–3 minutes. Add the tomato paste and chilli and cook for a further 3–4 minutes. Remove the pan from the heat and allow to cool. When the oil is completely cold, strain through a fine sieve into a jar, seal and store until needed.

Garnish: Mix together the coriander and Vietnamese mint leaves and reserve until needed.

Prepare the crispy shallot garnish according to the recipe (see Basics).

To Serve: Bring the soup back to a gentle simmer. Taste, and add lime juice, fish sauce and gula melaka until you achieve a pleasing balance of flavours.

Bring a pan of water to the boil. Place the dumplings in a lightly greased bamboo steamer basket. Cook in small batches, making sure they don't touch, or they will stick together. Cover with the lid and steam for 2–3 minutes, or until they are warm in the centre.

To serve, place 3 dumplings into each soup bowl and ladle over the hot soup. Garnish with a small handful of the fresh herbs and a pinch of crispy shallots. Drizzle over a teaspoon of spicy prawn oil and serve immediately.

Serves 6

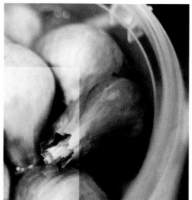

steamed duck dumplings

in a light asian broth with mushrooms, black beans, cucumber and ginger

Duck Dumplings

6 duck legs

2 litres (4 pints) Asian-style duck stock (see Basics)

8 fresh shiitake mushrooms, stalks removed, finely chopped

3 tablespoons finely chopped spring onions (scallions), white part only

2 tablespoons finely chopped coriander (cilantro) root

50 g (2 oz) chicken mousse (see Basics)

1 tablespoon light soy sauce

1 teaspoon sweet soy sauce (ketjap manis)

1 teaspoon sesame oil

salt and pepper

36 wonton skins, at room temperature

Light Asian Broth

2 litres (4 pints) duck cooking liquid

3 red bird's eye chillies

1 stalk lemongrass

20 g (¾ oz) fresh ginger

5 cloves garlic

1 bunch coriander (cilantro) root

½ teaspoon Sichuan peppercorns

4 star anise

100 ml (3½ fl oz) light soy sauce

2 tablespoons sweet soy sauce (ketjap manis)

4 egg whites

100 g (3½ oz) minced beef

salt and black pepper

Garnish

½ long cucumber, peeled

1 red Lombok chilli

5 spring onions (scallions), white part only

½ cup snow pea shoots

2 teaspoons salted black beans

½ cup coriander (cilantro) leaves

5 shiitake mushrooms, cut in quarters

1 small punnet enoki mushrooms, cut in half

Duck Dumplings: Preheat the oven to 160ºC (325ºF). Sear the duck legs in a hot dry frying pan until the skin turns golden brown and the fat starts to render, about 5 minutes. Transfer to a small, deep braising dish. Bring the duck stock to the boil and strain over the duck legs so they are completely covered. Cover the braising dish tightly with a lid or kitchen foil and cook in oven until the duck legs are tender, and the meat is starting to fall from the bone, about 1½ hours.

Remove from the oven and allow the duck legs to cool in the braising liquid. When they are completely cold, remove them from the liquid, carefully pull all the meat from the bones and break it into smallish pieces with your fingers. Strain the duck braising liquid and refrigerate for making the Asian broth.

Combine the cooked duck meat with the shiitake mushrooms, spring onions and coriander root. Add the chicken mousse and fold through so that it just binds the ingredients together. Mix in the two soy sauces and the sesame oil and season with salt and pepper.

Lay out 18 wonton skins on a dry flat surface and place a large teaspoon of the duck mixture in the centre of each one. Lightly brush around the edges of each wonton skin with water then top with the remaining 18 wonton skins. Use your fingers to press the edges together and seal the dumplings well. Use a 5 cm (2 in) cookie cutter to cut each dumpling into a neat circle. Refrigerate on a plastic wrap-lined tray until ready to cook – at least 20 minutes.

Infusion Stage

Light Asian Broth: Skim the chilled duck cooking liquid of all surface fat, then tip into a saucepan and gradually bring to the boil. Place the chillies, lemongrass, ginger, garlic, coriander, Sichuan peppercorns and star anise in the centre of a small piece of muslin cloth and tie the four corners together tightly so the contents can't escape. Place this spice bag in the stock, then add the two soy sauces and allow it all to infuse over a very gentle heat for about 20–30 minutes. Allow to cool completely before clarification.

Clarification Stage

Next, make a 'raft' to clarify the broth. Pour the stock into a large wide-based saucepan. In a small bowl thoroughly mix together the egg whites and minced beef, then add this mixture to the cool stock. It will immediately sink to the bottom. Now turn up the heat, which will make the 'raft' float to the surface, catching any impurities as it rises. Leave the 'raft' in the gently simmering stock for 10–12 minutes but do not allow it to boil. Turn off the heat and allow the stock to cool slightly.

Tip the pot slightly to one side and ladle out the stock, taking care not to break up the 'raft'. For the clearest broth, it is best to strain the clarified stock into a clean pot through muslin, which will remove any remaining impurities.

Garnish: Finely shred the cucumber and the chilli. Slice spring onions diagonally. Slice the snow pea shoots into bite-size pieces. Gently rinse the black beans under cold running water, then drain well and place in a mixing bowl with all the other garnish ingredients. Mix gently to combine.

To Serve: Reheat the broth and season to taste. Bring a pan of water to the boil. Place the duck dumplings in a lightly greased bamboo steamer basket. Cook in small batches making sure they don't touch or they will stick together. Cover with the lid and steam for about 5 minutes, or until they are hot in the centre.

To serve, place 3 dumplings into each soup bowl and ladle over the hot broth. Top with a small handful of the garnish and serve immediately.

Note: The broth makes enough for about 10 serves. Do not reduce the quantities, as it is not possible to clarify in smaller quantities.

Serves 6

wonton
dumplings

Wonton skins are incredibly versatile and I use them a great deal in my dishes. They are made from dough, a little bit like an Italian pasta dough, and may or may not include eggs. They can be white or yellow – I prefer to use the yellow ones. Traditionally, they are used in Chinese cooking to make little handmade dumplings.

I use wonton skins a lot to make all sorts of dumplings for soups, but not just in the traditional Chinese manner. The fillings can be incredibly diverse, ranging from seafood to chicken, duck or quail – or even oxtail – and lend themselves well to all sort of different Asian flavours.

Wonton dumplings can be made ahead of time and simply warmed through at the last minute, which makes them really good for dinner parties. Once you have prepared the dumplings, they should be briefly blanched in boiling water, which tightens the dough and seals the dumplings and helps prevent them going soggy. I always finish all pasta and dumplings in a steamer as I find it a much gentler process than boiling and helps the dumplings maintain their shape.

I also like to use wonton skins in a very untraditional way. Many Asian cuisines use very finely shredded vegetables as a deep-fried garnish, and I developed the idea of doing a similar thing with wonton skins. To make them, you stack a few wonton skins on top of one another and shred them as finely as possible with a very sharp knife. You are aiming to create very fine, hair-like strands of pasta, finer than vermicelli noodles if possible. The result when they are deep-fried is a delectably crispy little frizzle of golden strands.

Deep-fried whole wonton skins work very well as a crispy layer in layered dishes. They provide a delicious crunchy balance to smooth or creamy layers in between.

oxtail wonton dumplings
in sweet and sour broth with lime, chilli and shaved coconut

Oxtail

1.5 litres (2½ pints) veal stock (see Basics)

2 teaspoons olive oil

1.2 kg (2½ lb) oxtail, to yield about 500 g (1 lb) cooked meat

Soup Paste

200 g (7 oz) fresh ginger, peeled and finely chopped

160 g (5½ oz) fresh galangal, peeled and finely chopped

4 cloves garlic, peeled and finely chopped

30 g (1¼ oz) fresh turmeric, peeled and finely chopped

1 lemongrass stalk, white part only, finely chopped

5 fresh or frozen kaffir lime leaves

3 red bird's eye chillies

¼ cup coriander (cilantro) leaves

Sweet and Sour Broth

30 ml (1 fl oz) peanut oil

½ cup tamarind paste

1.5 litres (2½ pints) veal stock, reserved after cooking the oxtail

40 ml (1½ fl oz) gula melaka syrup (see Basics)

50 ml (1½ fl oz) lime juice

40 ml (1½ fl oz) fish sauce

Oxtail Wonton Dumplings

500 g (1 lb) cooked oxtail meat, roughly shredded

2 cloves garlic, finely chopped

3 shallots, finely chopped

1 lemongrass stalk, white part only, finely chopped

20 g (¾ oz) fresh ginger, finely chopped

5 medium spring onions (scallions), finely chopped

3 coriander (cilantro) roots, finely chopped

5 fresh lime kaffir leaves, finely chopped

1 red bird's eye chilli, finely chopped

zest of 1 orange, finely chopped

reduced braising liquid

3 tablespoons gula melaka syrup (see Basics), to taste

1 teaspoon sesame oil

36 wonton skins, at room temperature

Garnish

1 fresh coconut

1 long red chilli, cut into julienne strips

½ cup coriander (cilantro) leaves

Even people who would not normally order oxtail are seduced by this dish. The soft, almost buttery texture of the oxtail, bathed in a hot spicy broth produces a delectable contrast of textures, flavours and colours. If the soup is too spicy for your palate then use more veal stock and water.

Oxtail: Preheat the oven to 160°C (325°F). Bring the veal stock to the boil in a large saucepan skimming from time to time. Heat 2 teaspoons of oil in a large frying pan and brown the oxtail all over. Transfer the oxtail to a casserole dish and cover with hot veal stock. Cover with tight-fitting lid or kitchen foil and cook in oven for 2–3 hours, or until the meat is falling off the bone.

When the oxtail is cool enough to handle, remove it from the stock and pick the meat from the bones. Allow the meat to cool completely and reserve to make the dumplings. Strain the veal stock. Put 200 ml (7 fl oz) in a small saucepan and reduce by three-quarters to make a syrupy glaze (to add to the dumpling filling). Use the remaining stock to make the broth.

Soup Paste: Place the ginger, galangal, garlic, turmeric, lemongrass, lime leaves, chillies and coriander leaves in a food processor, or use a mortar and pestle, and grind to a fine paste.

Sweet and Sour Broth: Heat the peanut oil in a medium, non-reactive saucepan, add the soup paste and fry for about 15 minutes or until fragrant. Stir frequently to ensure the paste doesn't burn. Add the reserved veal stock and tamarind paste and bring to the boil. Lower the heat and simmer gently for a further 20 minutes. From time to time you will need to skim off any scum that floats to the top. Strain through a fine sieve and reserve until ready to serve.

Oxtail Wonton Dumplings: Place the oxtail meat in a large mixing bowl with the finely chopped garlic, shallots, lemongrass, ginger, spring onions, coriander, lime leaves, chilli, orange zest and the syrupy glaze. Mix gently until well combined. Season to taste with gula melaka and sesame oil.

Lay 18 wonton skins on a dry flat surface and place a generous teaspoon of the oxtail mixture in the centre of each one. Lightly brush around the edges of each wonton skin with water then top with the remaining 18 wonton skins. Use your fingers to press the edges together and seal the dumplings well. Use a 5 cm (2 in) cookie cutter to cut each dumpling into a neat circle. Refrigerate on a plastic wrap-lined tray until ready to cook – at least 20 minutes.

Garnish: Use a hammer to crack the coconut open. Use a small sharp knife or screwdriver to prise the coconut flesh away from the hard outer shell, there will still be a layer of dark skin attached. Place the coconut pieces over a naked flame, skin-side down, and toast for 3–4 minutes. Move the coconut constantly to make sure it doesn't burn. Allow to cool, and use a vegetable peeler or sharp knife to slice the coconut into long, thin shavings.

To Serve: Bring the soup to a simmer, add the prepared oxtail wontons and gently warm them through, about 3–5 minutes. Season the soup with gula melaka syrup, lime juice and fish sauce, adjusting until you get a nice balance of hot, salty and sour. Place 3 dumplings into each bowl then ladle over the soup. Garnish with the toasted coconut shavings, chilli and coriander leaves.

Note: Ask your butcher to chop the oxtail into pieces and to trim away any large lumps of fat.

Serves 6

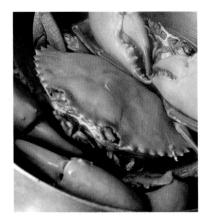

steamed crab wontons
with avocado, tomato, lime and black olive salad and sweet soy-chilli dressing

Crab Wontons

500 g (1 lb) freshly cooked crab meat

150 g (5 oz) blue eye mousse (see Basics)

¼ cup fresh chives, finely chopped

¼ cup fresh dill, finely chopped

salt and pepper

36 wonton skins, at room temperature

Avocado, Tomato, Lime and Black Olive Salad

2 vine-ripened tomatoes

1 ripe avocado, cut into 5 mm (¼ in) dice

1 baby fennel bulb, cut into 5 mm (¼ in) dice

1 small red onion, cut into 5 mm (¼ in) dice

1 lime, peeled, pith removed and cut into 5 mm (¼ in) dice

1 red Lombok chilli, deseeded

¼ cup black olives, pitted and sliced

¼ cup snow pea shoots, cut in half

1 tablespoon crispy shallot garnish (see Basics)

1 tablespoon pickled ginger (see Basics), finely chopped

Sweet Soy-Chilli Dressing

100 ml (3½ fl oz) olive oil

100 ml (3½ fl oz) sweet soy sauce (ketjap manis)

3 red bird's eye chillies, finely chopped

My head chef, Brendan McQueen, created this dish. It is a really well-thought-out dish that represents perfectly the style of the restaurant. The subtle sweetness of the crab meat works deliciously well with the salty, sour heat of the salad. We prefer to use mud crab when it is in season.

Crab Wontons: Place the crab meat and blue eye mousse in a large mixing bowl with the finely chopped herbs, and mix gently until well combined. Season with salt and pepper.

Lay 18 wonton skins on a dry flat surface and place a generous teaspoon of the crab mixture in the centre of each one. Lightly brush around the edges of each wonton skin with water then top with the remaining 18 wonton skins. Use your fingers to press the edges together and seal the dumplings well. Use a 9-cm (4-in) cookie cutter to cut each dumpling into a neat circle. Refrigerate on a plastic wrap-lined tray until ready to cook.

Avocado, Tomato, Lime and Black Olive Salad: Bring a small pot of water to the boil and blanch the tomatoes for around 10 seconds. Refresh in iced water for a further 10 seconds, then carefully peel away the skins. Cut each tomato into quarters, gently squeeze out the seeds and dice the flesh. Place the diced tomato in a large mixing bowl with the diced avocado, fennel, red onion and lime. Finely shred the chilli into longish strips and add to the salad with the olives, snow pea shoots, crispy shallots and pickled ginger. Mix the ingredients gently to combine.

Sweet Soy-Chilli Dressing: Stir together the olive oil, sweet soy sauce and chillies, and keep at room temperature until ready to serve.

To Serve: Bring a pan of water to the boil. Place the dumplings in a lightly greased bamboo steamer basket. Cook in small batches, making sure they don't touch, or they will stick together. Cover with the lid and steam for 2–3 minutes, or until they are warm in the centre.

Arrange 3 wontons in the centre of each plate. Dress the salad and place a small mound on top of the wontons. Serve immediately.

Serves 6

steaming

Steaming is one of my favourite ways of cooking. The food to be steamed is placed in a perforated container that is suspended above the water contained in a wok or saucepan below. The water is kept at a constant boil to create steam, which enters the steamer and cooks the food.

Steaming is a very gentle and controllable method of cooking that retains moisture and flavour in the food. This makes it perfect for cooking noodles, dumplings and other pasta dishes. It also works brilliantly with whole items: for instance, I love to steam little baby chickens and quail or baby fish like snapper or little red mullet. Many seafood items like oysters and scallops are also delicious steamed as their delicate flesh responds well to this gentle way of cooking.

If you use a well-flavoured stock, or aromatics in the steaming broth, it imparts a delicious flavour to the items being steamed. A stalk of lemongrass, for instance, will infuse a delicate piece of white fish with a lovely fragrance. The juices that fall back into the water from the item being steamed will also enrich the stock itself.

I like to use Asian-style steamers in my kitchen. I use traditional Chinese 'atmospheric' steamers. These are aluminium or stainless-steel steamers available from Asian stores. I also have a huge range of bamboo baskets that I use for steaming over woks. Bamboo baskets are really cheap and are incredibly versatile. They come in a wide variety of sizes, so will happily accommodate all sorts of food. Also, they stack on top of each other, which means as many as four or five dishes can be steamed simultaneously.

It is great fun to serve dishes at the table in bamboo steamers. I love the drama of removing the lid at the table, which immediately releases a cloud of aromatic steam into the air.

ocean trout ravioli
with wok-seared cress and snow pea shoots and spicy soy-butter dressing

Ocean Trout Ravioli

600 g (1¼ lb) ocean trout, skin and bones removed

1 egg white

5 medium spring onions (scallions), white part only, finely chopped

¼ cup coriander (cilantro) roots, finely chopped

1 lemongrass stalk, white part only, finely chopped

20 g (¾ oz) fresh ginger, peeled and finely chopped

4 fresh kaffir lime leaves, finely chopped

1 tablespoon lime juice

1½ tablespoons fish sauce

½ teaspoon grated palm sugar

2 teaspoons light soy sauce

500 g (1 lb) pasta dough (see Basics)

egg wash (see Basics)

Spicy Soy-Butter Dressing

3 shallots, finely sliced

20 g (¾ oz) fresh ginger, roughly chopped

1 clove garlic, roughly chopped

2 red bird's eye chillies, roughly chopped

150 ml (5 fl oz) verjuice

1 teaspoon white wine vinegar

60 ml (2 fl oz) thickened cream

300 g (10½ oz) diced unsalted butter, chilled

1 tablespoon light soy sauce

2 tablespoons sweet soy sauce (ketjap manis)

Cress Garnish

1 cup tatsoi (rosette bok choy)

1 cup snow pea shoots

1 tablespoon peanut oil

1 cup watercress

In this dish I have aimed for lighter, more subtle Asian flavours, using lemongrass, coriander and kaffir lime leaves. These fragrant, almost floral flavours work brilliantly with the delicate flesh of ocean trout, and the whole dish is brought to life by the spicy soy-butter dressing.

Ocean Trout Ravioli: Use a sharp knife to remove the bloodline from the trout. Cut two-thirds of the trout into 5 mm (¼ in) dice. Place the remaining third in a food processor and purée to a smooth paste with the egg white. Mix the paste and the diced trout together, then add the finely chopped spring onions, coriander root, lemongrass, ginger and lime leaves. Add the lime juice, fish sauce, palm sugar and light soy sauce and combine well. Roll mixture into 6 small balls, each weighing about 80 g (3 oz) and refrigerate for an hour.

Use a pasta maker to roll out the dough to the thinnest setting. Cut the long strip of dough in half to make it easier to work with, and lay out on a floured work surface Place the balls of trout filling at even intervals along the pasta dough. You should leave about 10 cm (4 in) between each portion. Lightly brush around the filling with a little egg wash then gently lay the second sheet of pasta on top. Use your fingers to press the two layers of dough firmly together around each mound of mixture to seal, ensuring no air is trapped inside. Use a 9 cm (4 in) cutter to cut each ravioli into a neat circle.

Bring a large pot of salted water to the boil and blanch the ravioli, one at a time for about 10–20 seconds, until they float to the top. Refresh in iced water to stop the cooking process then drain well and refrigerate on a plastic wrap-lined tray until ready to serve.

Spicy Soy-Butter Dressing: Place the shallots, ginger, garlic and chillies into a small non-reactive saucepan. Add the verjuice and white wine vinegar and bring to a gentle simmer. Cook for around 10 minutes until the mixture is reduced by two-thirds. Add the cream, return to a simmer and reduce by half again. Over a very low heat slowly whisk in the chilled butter, a few cubes at a time, until it is all thoroughly incorporated. Strain into a clean pan and add the two soy sauces to taste. Keep warm until needed.

Cress Garnish: Mix together the tatsoi and snow pea shoots and reserve until needed. Keep the cress separately.

To Serve: Bring a pan of water to the boil. Place the trout ravioli in a lightly greased bamboo steamer basket. Cook in small batches making sure they don't touch or they will stick together. Cover with the lid and steam for 2–3 minutes, or until they are warm in the centre.

When ready to cook the cress garnish, heat the tablespoon of peanut oil in a wok until it starts to smoke. Add the cress and toss in the hot oil until it starts to wilt.

To serve, place a little pile of wilted cress in the centre of each plate then carefully top with a ravioli. Drizzle with a little soy-butter sauce, garnish with the snow pea shoot mixture and serve straight away.

Note: The secret to making a butter sauce is in the temperature. If it is allowed to cool too much the sauce will set, but if it is too hot the sauce may split.

Serves 6

sweetbread tortellini
with chinese mushrooms, wilted spinach and sichuan pepper glaze

Sweetbread Tortellini

550 g (1 lb 2 oz) veal sweetbreads, soaked in water for at least 24 hours to remove any blood

100 g (3½ oz) flour

200 ml (7 fl oz) clarified butter

salt and pepper

5 red shallots, finely chopped

100 g (3½ oz) shiitake mushrooms, finely chopped

100 g (3½ oz) chicken mousse (see Basics)

3 tablespoons finely chopped chives

500 g (1 lb) pasta dough (see Basics)

100 ml (3½ fl oz) egg wash (see Basics)

Sichuan Glaze

1½ litres (2½ pints) veal stock (see Basics)

3 tablespoons Sichuan peppercorns

2 tablespoons Chinese black vinegar

Crispy Taro Garnish

1 small taro (or sweet potato), very finely shredded

1 litre (1¾ pints) vegetable oil

½ teaspoon icing (confectioners') sugar

½ teaspoon salt

2 tablespoons olive oil

150 g (5 oz) baby spinach

salt and pepper

6 sprigs chervil

Sweetbread Tortellini: Bring a large pot of water to the boil and blanch the sweetbreads for 1–2 minutes. Carefully remove the sweetbreads and refresh them in iced water to stop the cooking process. Pat the sweetbreads dry, peel away the skin and sinews and slice them into bite-size pieces.

Dust the sweetbread pieces with flour and shake off any excess. Heat 2 tablespoons of the clarified butter in a large frying pan and fry the sweetbreads until golden brown, about 10 minutes. Remove from the pan and drain on absorbent paper. Place the sweetbreads in a mixing bowl and season lightly with salt and pepper.

In another frying pan, heat another 2 teaspoons of clarified butter and sauté the shallots until soft, then add the shiitake mushrooms and cook for 2–3 minutes more. Remove the shallots and mushrooms from the pan and allow to cool. When cold, add them to the sweetbreads and mix together. Add the chicken mousse and chives and combine well. Season with salt and pepper and refrigerate until cold.

Use a pasta maker to roll the dough out to the thinnest setting. Lay out on a floured work surface and cut out 6 circles with a 12 cm (6 in) cutter. Place a tablespoon of the chilled sweetbread mix in the centre of each pasta disc. Brush lightly around one half of each tortellini with a little egg wash, then fold over to form a half-moon. Use your fingers to pinch the dough together and seal. Twist the two corners in until they touch and pinch them together using a little more egg wash. Repeat to make a total of 6 tortellini then return them to the refrigerator or freezer for about 5 minutes, just until the pasta begins to firm.

Meanwhile, bring a large pot of salted water to the boil. Place the chilled tortellini in the water a few at a time, and cook for 2–3 minutes. Remove the tortellini carefully and refresh in iced water to stop the cooking process. Drain well and refrigerate on a plastic wrap-lined tray until needed.

Sichuan Glaze: Put the veal stock in a non-reactive saucepan with the Sichuan peppercorns and reduce by three-quarters. Stir in the vinegar and keep warm until ready to serve.

Crispy Taro Garnish: To prepare the crispy taro, heat the vegetable oil to 180°C (350°F). Fry the shredded taro in small batches for 1–2 minutes, until it turns crispy. Drain on absorbent paper and allow to cool, then sprinkle with the icing sugar and salt. Store in a dry place until ready to use.

To Serve: Bring a pan of water to the boil. Place the sweetbread tortellini in a lightly greased bamboo steamer basket. Cook in small batches, making sure they don't touch, or they will stick together. Cover with the lid and steam for 5 minutes, or until they are hot in the centre.

Meanwhile cook the spinach garnish. Heat the olive oil in a large frying pan and sauté the spinach until it softens. Season with salt and pepper and divide between six plates. Arrange a tortellini on top of the spinach and top with a pinch of crispy taro and a sprig of chervil. Spoon the Sichuan glaze around the plate and serve straight away.

Serves 6

steamed scallop tortellini
with verjuice and citrus butter sauce, crispy leek and herb salad and yarra valley salmon eggs

Scallop Tortellini

400 g (14 oz)
fresh scallops
(including coral)
cleaned and cut
into quarters

200 g (7 oz) blue eye
mousse (see Basics)

2 tablespoons
chopped chives

salt and pepper

500 g (1 lb) pasta
dough (see Basics)

100 ml (3½ fl oz)
egg wash
(see Basics)

Crispy Leek and Herb Salad

2 leeks, white part only,
cut into julienne strips

1 litre (1¾ pints)
vegetable oil for frying

¼ cup fresh chervil

¼ cup fresh dill

¼ cup fresh chives,
cut into 4 cm
(1½ in) lengths

Verjuice and Citrus Butter Sauce

250 ml (7 fl oz) verjuice

½ lime, peel and juice

½ lemon, peel only

½ grapefruit, peel only

½ orange, peel only

50 ml (1¾ fl oz)
thickened cream

300 g (10½ oz) diced
unsalted butter, chilled

1 tablespoon
chopped chives

2 tablespoons Yarra
Valley salmon eggs
(or another good
quality salmon roe)

Scallop Tortellini: Place the scallops, blue eye mousse and chopped chives in a large bowl and gently mix together. Season very lightly with salt and pepper and place in the coldest part of your refrigerator to chill.

Use a pasta maker to roll the dough out to the thinnest setting. Lay the pasta out on a floured work surface and cut out 18 circles with a 9 cm (4 in) cookie cutter. Place a tablespoon of the chilled scallop mix in the centre of each pasta disc. Brush lightly around one half of each tortellini with a little egg wash, then fold over to form a half-moon. Use your fingers to pinch the dough together and seal. Twist the 2 corners in until they touch and pinch them together using a little more egg wash. Repeat to make a total of 18 tortellini then return them to the refrigerator or freezer for about 5 minutes, just until the pasta begins to firm.

Meanwhile, bring a large pot of salted water to the boil. Cook the chilled tortellini, a few at a time, until they float to the surface, around 2–3 minutes. Remove the tortellini carefully and refresh in iced water to stop the cooking process. Drain well and refrigerate on a plastic wrap lined tray until needed.

Crispy Leek and Herb Salad: In a medium-sized cooking pot heat the vegetable oil to 180°C (350°F). Fry the julienned leeks until golden brown, remove from the oil with a slotted spoon and drain on absorbent paper. Reserve until needed. In a separate bowl, gently mix together the herbs.

Verjuice and Citrus Butter Sauce: Put the verjuice into a small non-reactive saucepan with the four citrus peels and bring to a gentle simmer. Reserve the lime juice until later. Cook for 5–10 minutes, until nearly completely reduced. Add the cream, return to a simmer and reduce by half again. Remove the pan from the heat and slowly whisk in the chilled butter, a few cubes at a time, until it is all thoroughly incorporated. Strain into a clean pan and add the lime juice, chopped chives and salmon eggs. (The salmon eggs should only be added if you are going to serve straight away. Otherwise, keep the sauce warm until needed, and add the salmon eggs at the last minute.)

To Serve: Bring a pan of water to the boil. Place the tortellini in a lightly greased bamboo steamer basket. Cook in small batches, making sure they don't touch, or they will stick together. Cover with the lid and steam for 2–3 minutes, or until they are hot in the centre.

In a mixing bowl, gently combine the crispy leeks and fresh herbs, then place a little mound of this salad in the centre of each plate. Arrange 3 tortellini around the salad and drizzle with the butter sauce.

Note: The secret to making a butter sauce is in the temperature. If it is allowed to cool too much the sauce will set, but if it is too hot the sauce may split.

Serves 6

hand-made pasta

I love using hand-made pasta because it gives you control over the ingredients used. The best pasta can only be made from the best ingredients – the freshest free-range eggs and the best quality strong white flour. The resulting silky smooth texture and flavour is worth the effort (see Basics for recipe).

Although it doesn't take time to make the actual dough, it is a bit of a chore rolling it out through a pasta machine. But the dough is so incredibly versatile. You can cut the long sheets into noodles, or cut out little discs or squares for stuffing.

I use hand-made pasta in the Mod-Aus style! I make a traditional Italian pasta dough and then fill it in an unconventional way, with Asian-inspired fillings. For instance, I might make ravioli and fill them with ocean trout that is flavoured with kaffir lime, lemongrass and coriander and serve them with a spicy soy-butter dressing. Or I might fill tortellini with creamy sweetbreads enriched with earthy shiitake mushrooms and drizzled with a Sichuan pepper glaze.

Another benefit of making your own pasta dough is that you can add your own flavours to it. Traditional Italian pasta dough is often coloured with beetroot or spinach, for instance. I like to colour it with saffron or shiitake mushrooms or even green tea, and to spice up the flavour with Sichuan pepper or coriander seeds.

potato gnocchi gratin
with taleggio, pear and roasted walnuts

Potato Gnocchi

750 g (1 lb 10 oz)
potatoes, peeled

250 ml (9 fl oz) milk

100 g (3½ oz)
unsalted butter

200 g (7 oz) plain
(all-purpose) flour

2 eggs

salt and pepper

Taleggio Sauce

150 g (5oz) walnuts

500 ml (16 fl oz)
thickened cream

300 g 10 oz)
taleggio cheese

2 tablespoons finely
chopped chives

1 ripe pear

sea salt

250 g (9 oz)
parmesan cheese,
grated

6 sprigs of parsley
for garnish

Gnocchi: Bring a large pan of water to the boil and cook the potatoes until tender, 15–20 minutes. Drain well, then pass the potatoes through a sieve or potato ricer. Weigh the potatoes and reserve 500 g (1 lb), covered with plastic wrap, in a large mixing bowl. This is the correct weight of cooked potato you'll need.

Place the milk and butter in another saucepan and heat until the butter dissolves and the milk comes to the boil. Sift the flour into the hot milk and whisk until it has all been incorporated. Cook for 2–3 minutes, stirring continually with a wooden spoon. Transfer to an electric mixer and set the beaters to a low speed. Add the eggs, one at a time, making sure each one is incorporated well. Add the reserved potatoes and combine well. Taste, and season with salt and pepper if needed.

While the gnocchi mix is still warm, tip it onto a lightly floured work surface. Gently roll into long sausages about 2–2½ cm (¾–1 in) thick and cut into 2 cm (¾ in) lengths. Transfer the gnocchi to a lightly floured tray and refrigerate for about 15 minutes, or until they set firm.

Bring a large 5-litre (12 pint) saucepan of lightly salted water to the boil and tip in all the gnocchi. As they cook they will rise to the surface. Let them all rise, then turn off the heat and let them sit for 2–3 minutes. Lift the gnocchi out with a slotted spoon and plunge them into iced water. This will stop the cooking process and help them to set firm, which makes them easier to handle. Drain well and refrigerate on a plastic wrap-lined tray until needed.

Taleggio Sauce: Preheat the oven to 180°C (350°F). Roast the walnuts for about 3 minutes without allowing them to colour. Allow them to cool, then cut each walnut in half.

Cut the taleggio cheese into small dice and place in a small saucepan with the cream. Heat over a gentle flame, stirring until the cheese melts and the sauce reduces by a third, but do not allow it to boil. The sauce should be light and creamy, not heavy.

Peel and halve the pear and remove the core and stem. Cut each half into eight slices.

To Serve: Preheat the griller to its hottest temperature and bring a large pan of water to the boil.

Reheat the gnocchi in the boiling water, then drain them well and add to the warm sauce. Gently stir in the pear, roasted walnuts and chives, taste and adjust the seasoning if necessary.

Carefully spoon the gnocchi and some sauce into 6 individual, heatproof dishes. Sprinkle with parmesan cheese and cook under the griller until golden brown and bubbling. Decorate with a sprig of parsley and serve.

Serves 6

japanese-inspired oyster shooters

Shooter Mix

(Make 2 days ahead of time)

1 litre (1¾ pints) mirin

250 ml (9 fl oz) sake

75 ml (3 fl oz) Japanese rice wine vinegar

50 ml (1½ fl oz) light soy sauce

2 tablespoons wasabi powder

Oysters

18 oysters, freshly shucked

1 teaspoon wasabi paste

1 teaspoon pickled ginger (see Basics)

This is one of the most successful dishes I have ever created. It features on every menu and is always in demand. I 'invented' the dish after reading that Japanese wine tastes better once the alcohol has been burnt off. I tried it out and then started to experiment with the addition of extra flavours. This is the result, and I truly believe that the hot gush of wasabi combined with the saltiness of an oyster is pure ecstasy.

Shooter Mix: Put the mirin and sake into a non-reactive saucepan and bring to the boil. Once the wines reach boiling point, light a match and burn off the alcohol fumes. Be careful! Once the flames have subsided, remove from the heat and set aside to cool. Pour into a glass jug or decanter, and then add the rice wine vinegar, soy sauce and wasabi powder and stir until the wasabi has completely dissolved. Keep upright in the fridge for 24–48 hours, which allows the wasabi sediment to sink to the bottom. Strain off the clear liquid, being careful not to disturb the sediment at the bottom. Store in an airtight container in the refrigerator (it will keep for up to 1 week).

Oysters: Gently rinse each oyster in cold water to remove any grit from the shell. Cover with a damp cloth and refrigerate until needed.

To Serve: Place an oyster in each chilled shot glass and fill with shooter mix. Use a teaspoon to carefully bring the oyster to the top – it should float. Top each oyster with a small blob of wasabi paste and some pickled ginger and serve immediately for maximum impact.

Makes 18 Shooters

grilled tasmanian oysters
with prosciutto, spring onion, balsamic and parmesan

Oysters

18 large
Tasmanian oysters,
freshly shucked

Garnish

12 spring onions
(scallions), white
part only

100 g (3½ oz)
prosciutto,
finely sliced

100 ml (3½ fl oz)
balsamic vinegar

50 g (1½ oz)
shaved parmesan
cheese

Oysters: Gently rinse each oyster in cold water to remove any grit from the shell. Replace oysters on their half shells.

Garnish: Finely chop the spring onion and the prosciutto and place equal amounts on top of each oyster. Drizzle over a teaspoon of balsamic vinegar then top with a shaving of parmesan cheese.

To Serve: Preheat the grill to high. Place the oysters on a baking tray or the grill pan and grill for 1–2 minutes until the cheese turns golden brown. Serve straight away.

Serves 6

zucchini flower fritters stuffed with blue swimmer crab

with green chilli mayonnaise

Green Chilli Mayonnaise

2 teaspoons caraway seeds

2 teaspoons coriander seeds

7 long green chillies, halved, seeded and scraped

2 green bird's eye chillies, halved, seeded and scraped

1 cup baby spinach leaves

250 ml (9 fl oz) vegetable oil for frying

1 egg yolk

2 tablespoons white wine vinegar

1 teaspoon Dijon mustard

¼ cup coriander (cilantro) leaves

¼ cup mint leaves

250 ml (9 fl oz) olive oil

salt and freshly ground black pepper

Zucchini Flower Fritters

18 baby zucchini with flowers attached

¼ cup finely chopped chives

¼ cup finely chopped dill

¼ cup finely chopped coriander (cilantro) leaves

200 g (7 oz) blue eye mousse (see Basics)

250 g (9 oz) blue swimmer crab meat

1 litre (1¾ pints) peanut oil (for deep-frying)

plain (all-purpose) flour for dusting

900 ml (1½ pints) beer batter (see Basics)

Garnish

1 cup watercress, broken into small sprigs

lemon wedges

Green Chilli Mayonnaise: Lightly roast the caraway and coriander seeds until fragrant (3–4 minutes). Allow to cool, and grind to a fine powder in a spice grinder or with a mortar and pestle. Sieve to remove the husks. Chop all the chillies very finely.

Heat the vegetable oil to 180°C (350°F) and fry the spinach leaves until crispy. Drain on absorbent paper.

Place the egg yolk, white wine vinegar and Dijon mustard in a food processor. Add the ground spices, green chilli paste, the coriander and mint leaves and the fried spinach leaves. Blend to a smooth purée. Slowly add the olive oil until the mixture emulsifies and thickens. Season with salt and pepper and reserve.

Zucchini Flower Fritters: Carefully open each zucchini flower and pinch out the stamen. Trim to leave 3–4 cm (an inch or so) of the stem still attached to each flower.

Place the chopped herbs in a large mixing bowl with the blue eye mousse and blue swimmer crab and mix gently until well combined. Use a small spoon or piping bag to fill each zucchini flower about two-thirds full, leaving space for expansion during cooking. Twist the top of each flower to seal, place on a tray lined with plastic wrap and refrigerate until needed.

To Serve: When ready to fry the fritters, heat the peanut oil to 180°C (350°F) in a large pot or a small deep-fryer. Line a large flat tray with absorbent paper. Hold the zucchini and carefully dust each flower in the flour, shaking off any excess. Dip in the beer batter, then gently place in the hot oil – cook no more than 3 at a time – until the batter turns crisp and golden (about 2 minutes). Remove and drain on absorbent paper.

Place a large dollop of green chilli mayonnaise in the centre of each plate and stack 3 zucchini flowers around. Garnish with a few sprigs of watercress and serve immediately. Accompany with lemon wedges.

Serves 6

lime-cured cuttlefish
with sticky soy and bonito, tobikko, and crispy leek and seaweed salad

Bonito Dressing

1 tablespoon dashi

2 tablespoons bonito

2 tablespoons water

1 egg yolk

1 teaspoon Dijon mustard

3 tablespoons Japanese rice wine vinegar

250 ml (9 fl oz) peanut oil

1 teaspoon sweet soy sauce (ketjap manis)

juice of 1 lemon

Sticky Soy

See Basics

Crispy Leek and Seaweed Salad

1 litre (1¾ pints) vegetable oil for frying

2 leeks, white part only

salt

1 sheet of nori

Lime-Cured Cuttlefish

3 whole cuttlefish, around 500 g (1 lb) uncleaned weight

2 tablespoons lime juice

3 tablespoons mirin

4 teaspoons light soy sauce

1 tablespoon tobikko (wasabi flying fish roe)

While calamari is featured on nearly every second restaurant menu, for some reason cuttlefish is largely ignored. I don't know why, as it is quite simple to prepare and to cook. In this dish I love the way the lime juice curing mixture seems to bring out the smokiness of the bonito and salty-sweetness of the soy sauce and seaweed. It is also very simple to adjust the quantities to suit individual tastes.

Bonito Dressing: Put the dashi, bonito and water in a small saucepan and heat gently until dissolved. Mix to a smooth paste, remove from the heat and allow to cool. Put the egg yolk, mustard and rice wine vinegar into a food processor with the dashi paste and blend to a smooth purée. Gradually add the peanut oil until the mixture emulsifies and thickens. Add the sweet soy sauce and lemon juice and stir in thoroughly. Store in the refrigerator.

Sticky Soy: Prepare according to instructions (see Basics).

Crispy Leek and Seaweed Salad: In a medium pot or small deep-fryer heat the vegetable oil to 180°C (350°F). Cut the leek in half, lengthwise, then shred it finely into hair-like strands. Fry in the hot oil until it turns golden brown, then remove with a slotted spoon and drain on absorbent paper. Allow to cool, then season with salt and store in a dry place until needed.

Cut the nori sheet in half and shred it finely into hair-like strands. Store in a dry place until needed.

Lime-Cured Cuttlefish: Hold the head of the cuttlefish in one hand, pull away and discard the tentacles. Use a sharp knife to cut open the body. Remove the cuttlebone and guts and discard. Hold the cuttlefish under cold running water, rinse well and rub away the coloured membrane that covers the body and tentacles. This can be quite hard work, but is necessary as otherwise the cuttlefish will be tough and chewy. Dry the cuttlefish well, then slice crosswise, as finely as possible.

Place the cuttlefish in a large deep bowl and add the lime juice, mirin and soy sauce. Mix well so the cuttlefish is thoroughly coated and leave to cure for 2–3 minutes. Once cured, the flavours should be well balanced and the cuttlefish should be tender and not too chewy.

To Serve: Arrange 3 Chinese spoons on each plate (you'll need 18 in total) and drizzle a small amount of sticky soy into the bottom of each one. Divide the cuttlefish mixture between the spoons evenly, pour over a tablespoon of bonito dressing and top with a small amount of tobikko.

Top each spoon with a small amount each of the crispy leek and nori.

Serves 6

cured salmon stack

with lattice chips, yarra valley salmon pearls, crème fraîche and citrus oil

Cured Salmon

800 g (1¾ lb) Tasmanian salmon fillet, skin on

150 g (5 oz) yellow rock sugar

75 g (3 oz) sea salt

½ cup fresh dill, roughly chopped

4 fresh kaffir lime leaves, finely shredded

25 ml (1 fl oz) vodka

Lattice Chips

5 large desirée potatoes, peeled

1 litre (2 pints) vegetable oil

Citrus Oil

1 small lemon

1 small lime

1 small orange

100 ml (3½ fl oz) pure olive oil

Garnish

200 ml (7 fl oz) crème fraîche

¼ cup fresh dill

6 teaspoons Yarra valley salmon eggs, or another good quality salmon roe

Everyone I know loves salmon and there's definitely a sense of satisfaction in curing it yourself. It's not hard to do and this recipe – I think of it as a modern gravalax – makes a great start to any dinner or a delicious light lunch dish. It's visually stunning, and each component contributes its own flavour and texture. I particularly love the salty explosion of salmon eggs in the mouth.

Cured Salmon: Remove the pin bones from the salmon fillet and scrape away any fish scales. Trim neatly, removing any fins or straggly pieces. Leave the skin on the salmon.

In a mortar and pestle, pound the yellow rock sugar roughly so that it breaks down into large crystals. Tip into a large bowl and mix with the salt, dill and kaffir lime leaves. Lastly, add the vodka and mix everything together well.

Tip the curing mixture into a deep tray, large enough to accommodate the salmon fillet. Lay the salmon on top of the curing mix, skin side up, and cover with plastic wrap. Refrigerate for 36 hours.

Lattice Chips: Set the mandolin to the corregated blade. Slice the potatoes in a criss-cross manner to form a lattice of each slice. If you don't have a mandolin, you won't get the same lattice effect. Instead, use a very sharp knife to slice the potatoes as finely as you can. Either way, you will need about 30 slices. Heat the oil in a medium-sized saucepan to 180°C (350°F). Fry the potatoes a few at a time until golden brown and crispy, about 3–4 minutes. Remove them from the oil and drain on absorbent paper. Store in a dry place.

Citrus Oil: Preheat the oven to 100°C (240°F). Peel the citrus fruits and carefully remove any pith left on the skin (any pith left may make the oil bitter). Spread the citrus peelings out evenly on a baking tray and place them in the oven until they turn crisp and dry, preferably overnight. Place the dried citrus peel into a blender with the olive oil and blitz until smooth. Tip into a sealable jar and leave to infuse for at least 24 hours.

Garnish: Tip the crème fraîche into a large mixing bowl and whisk until it thickens. Spoon it into a piping bag fitted with a small nozzle and refrigerate until ready to serve.

To Serve: Take the salmon out of the cure and wipe it clean and dry with kitchen paper. Using a very sharp knife, slice the salmon thinly on a 45° angle. Start at the tail end and work your way along the fillet, until you have 24 even slices. Place each slice on a lattice chip and top with a little crème fraîche and a sprig of dill.

Pipe a ziz-zag of crème fraîche onto each plate. In the centre of each plate, carefully stack 4 of the prepared lattice chips. Spoon a teaspoon of the salmon eggs around each plate and garnish with sprigs of dill. To finish, drizzle citrus oil around the plate and top each stack with the remaining lattice chip.

Serves 6

curing

I use two methods of curing in the restaurant – slow curing which can take several days, and quick curing which takes anywhere from a few seconds to a few minutes. It is a delicious method of 'cooking' food – typically fish and seafood.

Slow curing tends to be used for whole fillets of large fish, such as salmon, trout or swordfish. A mixture of sugar, salt and aromatic spices is rubbed all over the flesh and left to work its magic. Some of my favourite aromatics are whole peppercorns and coriander seeds and shredded kaffir lime leaves. The result is a lovely soft butter texture with a lovely balanced flavour of sweet saltiness and underlying spice.

Quick curing is often known as ceviche, and is a very fast method that works well on smaller items – finely sliced or shredded fish and seafood, for instance. The curing mix always uses citrus juices mixed with other seasonings and aromatics, and it is the acid that 'cooks' the flesh. In the restaurant we will often quick-cure items to order. For instance, very finely shredded calamari or cuttlefish are delicious 'cooked' in a Japanese-inspired lime juice cure (see page 49), while salmon is really brought to life in an Asian-influenced vodka cure (see page 50).

tuna sashimi and wonton stack
with wasabi crème fraîche, nashi pear and mustard cress and sticky soy

Tuna Sashimi	Wasabi Crème Fraîche	Wontons	Nashi Pear and Mustard Cress Salad
500 g (1 lb) sashimi-quality tuna, skin removed	150 ml (5 fl oz) crème fraîche	1 litre (1¾ pints) vegetable oil	1 nashi pear
	2 teaspoons wasabi paste	30 wonton skins, cut down to 5 cm x 5 cm (2 in x 2 in), at room temperature	100 g (3½ oz) mustard cress, or any Asian baby cress
Sticky Soy			
3 tablespoons sticky soy (see Basics)			50 g (2 oz) pickled ginger (see Basics), cut into julienne strips

This is an exciting and fun kind of restaurant dish as it doesn't need cutlery. I love the texture of the crispy wontons with the smoothness of the tuna, and the peppery cress and hot wasabi really lift it out of the ordinary. It is visually stunning but really easy to prepare.

Tuna Sashimi: Use a very sharp knife to remove the bloodline from the tuna, and cut into 24 even bite-sized slices. Refrigerate until needed.

Wasabi Crème Fraîche: Whisk together the crème fraîche and wasabi paste until the mixture thickens. Refrigerate until ready to serve.

Wontons: Heat the vegetable oil to 180°C (350°F) in a medium saucepan. Fry the wonton skins, a couple at a time, for about 30 seconds on each side. Make sure they stay flat in the cooking oil. Remove from the oil and drain on absorbent paper.

Nashi Pear and Mustard Cress Salad: Peel the nashi pear and cut into julienne strips. Don't cut the pear too far in advance or it will oxidise and discolour.

To Serve: Lay out 24 fried wonton skins on a clean work surface, keeping 6 to one side to form 'lids'. On each wonton, place a slice of tuna, a pinch each of nashi pear, mustard cress and pickled ginger and a teaspoon of wasabi crème fraîche. Neatly stack 4 prepared wontons on each serving plate, one on top of the other. Complete each stack with a reserved wonton 'lid'. Drizzle a large swirl of sticky soy around the plate and serve straight away.

Serves 6

My style of cooking relies on flavoured dressings and oils rather than heavy stocks and sauces. I love to use infused oils for the colour and intensity of flavour they can add to a dish – at any one time in the restaurant we might have as many as 10 different flavoured oils in use.

Sometimes oils are flavoured with a purée of fresh herbs, but more often I will infuse them with aromatics for a more refined flavour hit. They are incredibly versatile and can be incorporated into dressings, mayonnaises, sauces or simply used as a garnish to drizzle over food before serving.

Different oils have different qualities and so work well with different types of flavours and in different types of dishes. Here are some of my favourites:

peanut oil

I mainly use this for deep-frying and wok-frying. It is also good with peanut-based dishes. I also use peanut oil for Asian-spiced mayonnaises where extra-virgin olive oil would be too 'grassy'. I particularly like to infuse peanut oil with spicy roasted peanuts. The spicy nuts can be used in the dish itself and the infused oil used to flavour all sorts of dressings and emulsifications.

oils & oil infusions

sesame oil
This is a very strongly flavoured oil made from ground sesame seeds. It needs to be used very sparingly or it will overpower a dish. I tend to cook the sesame oil before using it, as it is quite volatile. Sesame oil adds a lovely toasty nutty flavour to food.

vegetable oil
I use this for deep- and shallow-frying. It has a neutral flavour.

olive oil
Another oil I use all the time in my kitchen that lends itself particularly well to infusions. I tend to use olive oil in non-Asian dishes. It is less strongly flavoured than extra-virgin olive oil, which means it takes on other flavours really well. I use olive oil for dressings and emulsifications and for pan-frying fish. I love to infuse it with parmesan cheese or rosemary and garlic or chillies. It is also delicious infused with whole sticks of cinnamon – the resulting oil is lovely to use in desserts.

extra-virgin olive oil
A really good quality, well-flavoured extra-virgin olive oil really needs nothing else really to improve it. It is perfect for dressing European-style salads, or just for drizzling over food before serving.

western australian sardines
dressed with roasted peanuts, hot mint, chilli and lemon juice

Sardines

24 whole Western Australian sardines

120 ml (4 fl oz) clarified butter or ghee

50 g (2 oz) plain (all-purpose) flour

Roasted Peanut and Chilli Dressing

200 ml (7 fl oz) peanut oil

70 g (3 oz) roasted unsalted peanuts, roughly chopped

2 red bird's eye chillies, finely chopped

salt

50 ml (2 fl oz) sweet soy sauce (ketjap manis)

70 ml (3 fl oz) balsamic vinegar

juice of 1 lemon

¼ cup Vietnamese mint leaves, roughly chopped

¼ cup coriander (cilantro) leaves, roughly chopped

Salad

1 red oak leaf lettuce, outer leaves removed

1 green oak leaf lettuce, outer leaves removed

juice of 1 lemon

Garnish

6 small sprigs Vietnamese mint

This was my very first 'signature' dish. It relies heavily on balance, as one dominating flavour will ruin the dish. Really, it is all in the dressing – the combination of Italian balsamic vinegar and Indonesian sweet soy sauce is certainly 'out there', but it works!

Sardines: Rinse the sardines gently under cold running water. Use a very sharp knife to cut the head from each sardine. Slice open the belly and remove the guts, ribcage and backbone, then flatten the sardines out to butterfly them. Snip away the fins, but leave the tail attached. Don't rinse the sardines again as they will lose flavour. Refrigerate until ready to fry.

Roasted Peanut and Chilli Dressing: Put the oil in a small frying pan with the chopped peanuts and chillies. Heat the oil to 180°C (350°F) and fry the peanuts and chillies until golden brown. Strain the oil into a clean container and tip the chilli-peanut mixture onto absorbent paper. Season the chilli-peanut mixture with salt and leave to cool.

In a mixing bowl, whisk together the sweet soy sauce and balsamic vinegar. Taste to ensure that there is a perfect balance of sweet and sour. Add the cold infused oil and the lemon juice and stir in gently without whisking. Add the peanuts and chillies to the dressing, with the chopped Vietnamese mint and coriander. Use fairly promptly so that the dressing maintains its texture and flavour balance.

To Serve: Mix together the salad leaves in a large bowl and toss lightly with lemon juice.

Heat a tablespoon of clarified butter in a large frying pan until it bubbles. Dust the sardines in flour, shaking off any excess. Fry the sardines in batches skin side down, for about 30 seconds, or until they are golden brown. Turn carefully and fry for 30 seconds on the other side. Drain on absorbent paper and keep warm. Heat more clarified butter and fry the remaining sardines.

Place a small mound of lettuce leaves in the centre of each plate and arrange 4 sardines around it, like spokes in a wheel. Drizzle a little roasted peanut and chilli dressing over the sardines and garnish with a sprig of Vietnamese mint.

Note: Use the best and freshest sardines available. Garfish is a good replacement.

Serves 6

crayfish, mango and avocado salad

with soy and bonito dressing, wasabi flying fish roe and crispy seaweed garnish

Crayfish

1 live crayfish
(rock lobster),
about 1.5 kg (3 lb)

peel of 1 orange,
roughly sliced

peel of 1 lemon,
roughly sliced

½ head celery, sliced

1 teaspoon whole
coriander seeds

½ medium bunch
coriander (cilantro)

½ medium bunch dill

250 ml (9 fl oz) rice
wine vinegar

pinch of sea salt

Mango and Avocado Salad

1 large or two small
heads of white witlof

1 tablespoon hazelnut oil

salt and black pepper

1 large ripe mango

1 ripe avocado

squeeze of lemon juice

100 g (3½ oz)
somen noodles

1 tablespoon peanut oil

Soy and Bonito Dressing

½ tablespoon dried dashi

2 tablespoons dried
bonito flakes

1 tablespoon
very hot water

1 egg yolk

1 teaspoon Dijon mustard

40 ml (1½ fl oz)
Japanese rice wine vinegar

2 teaspoons sweet soy
sauce (ketjap manis)

150 ml (5 fl oz) peanut oil

juice of ½ lemon

Crispy Seaweed Garnish

1 litre (1¾ pints)
vegetable oil,
for frying

2 leeks, white part
only, cut into about
6 cm lengths

salt

1 sheet of nori

3 teaspoons
tobbiko (wasabi
flying fish roe)

Crayfish: To kill the crayfish place it in the freezer for 1 hour, where it will go to sleep. Place the orange and lemon peel, celery, coriander seeds, fresh herbs, vinegar and salt in a large 5-litre cooking pot. Fill three-quarters full with water and bring to the boil. Plunge the crayfish into the rapidly boiling stock, then cover with a lid and turn off the flame. Let the crayfish sit in the hot stock for 25 minutes, then drain and allow it to cool. Once the crayfish reaches room temperature, refrigerate until completely chilled.

When the crayfish is cold, pull the tail section away from the head. Use a pair of sharp scissors to cut the inner shell of the tail to get at the meat. Carefully draw the tail flesh out in one piece and reserve. Remove the legs from the body. Break at each joint then pick out the meat using a skewer or crab-pick. Cover and refrigerate both tail and leg meat until ready to assemble the final dish.

Mango and Avocado Salad: Slice off the base of the witlof then pull away the individual leaves, discarding any which are damaged. Finely slice each the leaves lengthwise and place in a mixing bowl. Dress lightly with hazelnut oil and season with salt and pepper.

Slice off each mango 'cheek' and use a large spoon to carefully scoop out the flesh. Dice into bite-size pieces and reserve. Slice the avocado in half lengthwise, remove the stone and carefully scoop out the flesh. Dice into bite-size pieces, toss in a little lemon juice to stop it browning and reserve.

Bring a small pot of salted water to the boil and cook the somen noodles until al dente (about 3–4 minutes). Tip into a colander and refresh under cold water to stop the noodles cooking further. Drain well, then tip into a bowl, toss with the peanut oil and reserve.

Soy and Bonito Dressing: Dissolve the dashi and the bonito flakes in the hot water to form a paste. Allow to cool completely. Place the egg yolk, mustard, vinegar, sweet soy sauce and prepared dashi paste in a food processor. Blend to a purée, then slowly add the peanut oil until the mixture emulsifies and thickens. Stir in the lemon juice and reserve.

Crispy Seaweed Garnish: In a medium pot or small deep-fryer heat the vegetable oil to 180°C (350°F). Cut the leek in half, lengthwise, then shred it finely into hair-like strands. Fry in the hot oil until it turns golden brown, then remove with a slotted spoon and drain on absorbent paper. Allow to cool, then season with salt and store in a dry place until needed.

Cut the nori sheet in half and shred it finely into hair-like strands. Reserve until needed.

To Serve: Using a very sharp knife, slice the crayfish tail meat into rounds. Depending on the size, it should yield between 18 and 24 slices.

Roughly chop the crayfish leg meat and put in a large mixing bowl with the witlof, mango, avocado and somen noodles. Pour over the dressing and combine gently. Season with sea salt and freshly ground black pepper.

Place three Chinese soup spoons on each plate and divide the salad equally between them. Top each little mound of salad with a slice of crayfish tail meat followed by a teaspoon of wasabi flying fish roe. Finish with a pinch each of fried leek and nori.

Serves 6

deep-frying

In my view, texture is one of the most important aspects of a dish, and I find that balancing the textures is as important as balancing flavours. Deep-frying is used in Asian cooking in the same way as it is used in the West – to add a delicious crunchiness and crispness to food.

In these health-conscious days, people are often a little scared of the idea of deep-frying, and it is not something that you would want to do every day! But on the plus side, do bear in mind that many nutritionists suggest that deep-frying food at hot temperatures means that it absorbs less fat than if it is shallow-fried.

If you have a deep fryer, then of course the process is made much easier, but you can achieve exactly the same result using a saucepan or a wok, in the Asian manner. As for the oil you choose, then that depends on the type of dish you are cooking. Different South East Asian countries use different oils by choice, ranging from coconut oil to ghee or liquid pork fat. But in Asia, as in the West, there is now a swing towards using healthier poly- and mono-unsaturated oils (olive oil, although a very healthy option, doesn't suit for deep-frying Asian-influenced foods). I prefer to use vegetable oil or peanut oil, depending on the dish.

Dipping items such as vegetables, fish and other pieces of seafood in batter before deep-frying, creates a crisp shell which is also delicious. And when it comes to meat, poultry and fish, anything that has a skin fries up really well.

I will often use a deep-fried garnish to add a crispy component to a dish – herbs, shredded vegetables and wonton skins all work really well. They look really attractive and provide height and drama as well as crunchiness.

I also like to deep-fry as the final part in a multi-stage cooking process. For example, food that has been first steamed or poached in a stock can then be deep-fried. Terrific examples of this are the Red Roast Baby Chicken (see page 111) and Crispy Fried Pork Hock (see page 121).

chilli salt squid
with asian herb salad and
palm sugar-lime juice dressing

Chilli Salt

½ cinnamon stick

50 g (1½ oz)
sea salt flakes

1 teaspoon whole
Sichuan peppercorns

1 teaspoon whole
coriander seeds

1 star anise

1 teaspoon dried
chilli flakes

1 cardamom pod

**Palm Sugar and
Lime Juice Dressing**

50 ml (1½ fl oz)
lemon juice

50 ml (1½ fl oz)
lime juice

50 g (1½ oz) palm
sugar, coarsely grated

50 ml (1½ fl oz)
olive oil

Asian Herb Salad

½ cup mint leaves

½ cup coriander
(cilantro) leaves

½ cup watercress sprigs

½ cup Thai basil leaves

1 medium red onion

1 long cucumber, peeled

Garnish

4 cloves garlic, finely sliced

40 g (1½ oz) fresh ginger,
peeled and finely sliced

1 red Lombok
chilli, finely sliced

1 litre (1¾ pints)
peanut oil for frying

fish sauce to taste,
about 1 teaspoon
per person

Squid

3 medium squid,
about 1 kg
uncleaned weight

150 g (5 oz)
rice flour

This is a signature dish at my restaurant, and represents all that I aim to achieve in my food. It combines sweet, sour, hot and salty flavours and the fried squid and crispy garnish provide a delicious crunch. I urge you to use the best quality, freshest ingredients and this dish will sing to you!

Chilli Salt: Roughly break up the cinnamon stick by hand and place in a mixing bowl with the other ingredients. Toss together well. Dry-fry over a low heat until fragrant, about 5 minutes, tossing constantly to avoid burning. Remove from the heat and allow to cool. Grind to a powder using a mortar and pestle or spice grinder.

Palm Sugar and Lime Juice Dressing: Put the citrus juices and grated palm sugar into a mixing bowl and whisk until the sugar has dissolved. Add the olive oil, whisk well and reserve. The dressing should be a nice balance of tangy, sweet and sour.

Asian Herb Salad: Place all the herbs in a large mixing bowl. Halve the red onion lengthways and slice finely into semicircles. Cut the cucumber in half lengthwise, remove the seeds and slice it finely. Combine all the salad ingredients gently, cover with plastic wrap and keep refrigerated until ready to serve.

Garnish: Heat the peanut oil to 180°C (350°F) in a wok or a small deep-fryer. Fry garlic, ginger and chilli separately until crispy and golden brown. Remove from the oil with a slotted spoon and drain on absorbent paper. Reserve separately until ready to serve. Allow the oil to cool and keep for frying the squid.

Squid: To prepare the squid, twist and pull the tentacles away from the body – the guts and head will come away too. Cut the tentacles off, just below the head, then pop out the 'beak' and discard it. Draw the piece of transparent cartilage out from the body. Carefully peel away the wings and skin. Wash the remaining tube, then dry it well and slice into thin rings. Cut the tentacles into bite-size pieces. Refrigerate until ready to fry.

To Serve: Reheat the peanut oil to 180°C (350°F) in a wok or deep-fryer. Dry the calamari and dust well with rice flour, making sure the calamari rings are completely coated. Shake off any excess flour and fry in small batches until a light golden brown, about 3–4 minutes. Drain on absorbent paper.

Tip the hot calamari into a mixing bowl and season to taste with the Chilli Salt. Add the calamari to the salad ingredients together with the crispy garnish. Toss with enough citrus dressing to lightly coat the leaves and season to taste with fish sauce.

Arrange a high mound of salad on each plate and drizzle a little extra dressing around the plate.

Serves 6

tempura fried quail
with green papaya, pomelo and peanut salad, spiced salt and sweet soy

Tempura Fried Quail

6 x 200 g (7 oz) jumbo quail

2 litres (1¾ pints) peanut oil for frying

½ cup plain (all-purpose) flour

300 ml (10½ fl oz) chilled tempura batter (see Basics)

Sweet Soy Dressing

50 ml (1½ fl oz) sweet soy sauce (ketjap manis)

25 ml (¾ fl oz) light soy sauce

25 ml (¾ fl oz) Japanese soy sauce (tamari)

Garnish

6 teaspoons prickly ash (see Basics)

3 limes, cut in halves

Green Papaya, Pomelo and Peanut Salad

1 pomelo (or large pink grapefruit)

50 g (2 oz) rice-stick noodles

1 tablespoon peanut oil

2 tablespoons fish sauce

1 teaspoon pickled ginger (see Basics), cut into julienne strips

1 red Lombok chilli, finely shredded

1 cup Vietnamese mint leaves

1 cup coriander (cilantro) leaves

2 tablespoons finely chopped roasted peanuts

12 cherry tomatoes, halved

150 g (5 oz) pickled green papaya (see Basics)

2 tablespoons crispy shallot garnish (see Basics)

juice of 2 limes

This is one of my very favourite dishes, and another one that lends itself to dramatic presentation. In the restaurant we serve each diner with all the individual components of the dish arranged on a large white plate topped with a piece of banana leaf and a sheet of Chinese newspaper (see Note). It looks simply stunning and tastes just as good as it looks.

Tempura Fried Quail: Trim the quail of their necks and wing tips, then split them in half down the backbone and flatten out. Partially bone the quail by slicing out the breastplate (sternum) and the wishbone. Be careful not to cut through the flesh and skin of the bird. Clean the birds and pat them dry.

Bring a large pan of water to the boil. Place the quails in a lightly greased bamboo steamer basket, and steam, for 6–7 minutes. Remove from the basket and allow to cool. Refrigerate the quails for at least an hour before you fry them.

Sweet Soy Dressing: Whisk the three soy sauces together and keep until needed.

Green Papaya, Pomelo and Peanut Salad: Peel the pomelo and use a sharp knife to slice out each segment from its casing.

Bring a small pot of water to the boil. Add the rice-stick noodles, then remove the pot from the heat and allow the noodles to soak in the hot water for 3–4 minutes, or until they are tender. Refresh under cold water, then drain thoroughly. Tip the noodles into a mixing bowl and stir through the peanut oil and 1 tablespoon of the fish sauce.

Assemble and prepare the remaining salad ingredients, and keep until ready to serve.

To Serve: In a medium saucepan or deep-fryer heat the peanut oil to 180ºC (350ºF). Dust each quail lightly with flour, shaking off any excess. Dip into the tempura batter and deep-fry, 2 at a time, until crispy and golden brown, 4–5 minutes. Remove the quail from the oil with a slotted spoon, dry on absorbent paper and cut in half lengthwise.

In a large bowl, mix all the salad ingredients together. Pour over the lime juice and remaining 1 tablespoon fish sauce and toss well. Taste for flavour balance, and adjust if needed.

Place a mound of salad in the centre of each plate and stack prickly ash and the 2 halves of quail on top. Serve with lime halves and little dishes of prickly ash and the sweet soy dressing.

Note: A very attractive way of presenting this dish is the way we do it in the restaurant. On each large white plate lay a square of Chinese newspaper, topped with a square of banana leaf – each about 13 x 13 cm (5 x 5 in). Place a mound of salad on top of the banana leaf and stack the two halves of quail on top. Next to the quail place little individual dishes of prickly ash and dressing. Wrap the halves of lime in a small square of muslin, tied into a neat tight knot to trap the pips as you squeeze.

Serves 6

drunken chicken cups
with deep-fried asian coleslaw and chilli mayonnaise

1 x 1.6 kg (3 lb)
free-range
organic chicken

Poaching Liquor

1.5 litres
(2½ pints) sake

150 ml (5 fl oz)
cane sugar syrup
or glucose

1 pandan leaf

Chilli Mayonnaise

20 g (¾ oz) fresh
ginger, peeled and
finely chopped

2 cloves garlic,
finely chopped

3 red bird's eye
chillies, finely
chopped

1 egg yolk

50 ml (1½ fl oz)
Japanese rice
wine vinegar

250 ml (9 fl oz)
peanut oil

zest and juice
of 1 lime

Asian Coleslaw

1 bunch Chinese
broccoli, leaves only,
finely shredded

1 carrot, peeled
and finely shredded

½ medium sweet
potato, peeled and
finely shredded

1 bunch kalium, leaves
only, finely shredded

40 g (1½ oz) fresh
ginger, peeled and
finely shredded

15 wonton
skins, chilled

1 lotus root,
peeled

1 litre (1¾ pints)
vegetable oil
for frying

1 teaspoon icing
(confectioners')
sugar, sifted

salt

Garnish

2 iceberg lettuces

3 fresh kaffir
lime leaves

2 tablespoons
roasted peanuts

¼ cup Vietnamese
mint leaves,
finely shredded

While visiting Hong Kong I had the opportunity of visiting a restaurant kitchen and working with a Chinese grandmother! She showed me how to cook drunken chicken in the traditional Chinese way. I like to season the crisp fried vegetables used in the Asian coleslaw with salt and sugar. This makes for really exciting flavours and the crispness of the coleslaw acts as a perfect counterpoint to the jelly-like texture of the chicken.

As with all recipes, select the best and freshest ingredients. When choosing your chicken, make sure it is free of blemishes and the skin is not torn.

Drunken Chicken: Bring a large saucepan of water to the boil. Blanch the chicken in the boiling water for about 10 seconds, then refresh in ice-cold water. This process will tighten the skin across the breast and bring out any excess fat. Repeat three times, taking care not to tear the skin of the chicken at any time.

Place the sake, sugar syrup and pandan leaf in a large 5-litre cooking pot and bring to the boil. Add the chicken to this poaching liquor and return to simmer. Cover the pan, lower the heat and poach gently for 45 minutes. To test if the chicken is cooked, pierce the leg with a thin skewer and if the juices run clear the bird is cooked.

Remove the pan from the heat and leave the chicken to cool in its poaching liquor. When completely cold, refrigerate and leave for 24 hours to ensure the flesh is 'drunken'. Make sure not to tear the skin when handling.

Chilli Mayonnaise: Place the finely chopped ginger, garlic and chillies in a mortar and pestle and pound to a fine paste. Scrape the paste into a food processor and add the egg yolk and vinegar and blend slowly to a purée. With the motor still running, slowly add the peanut oil until the mixture emulsifies and thickens. Add the lime zest and juice and a tablespoon of hot water (this will help to stabilise the mayonnaise and stop it splitting). Refrigerate until needed.

Asian Coleslaw: Prepare the Chinese broccoli, carrot, sweet potato, kalium and ginger for the coleslaw and reserve separately until ready to fry. Slice the chilled wonton skins into long thin hair-like strands and store on a separate tray ready for frying.

Use a mandolin or very sharp knife to slice the lotus root as thinly as possible and reserve separately.

In a medium-size (3-litre) cooking pot heat the vegetable oil to 180°C (350°F). Line several large trays with absorbent paper to drain the fried vegetables. Fry each ingredient (the shredded Chinese broccoli, carrot, sweet potato, ginger, wonton skins, kalium leaves and sliced lotus root) separately, until crispy and golden. The kalium will only take a few seconds. Remove from the oil with a slotted spoon and drain on absorbent paper, ensuring that each ingredient is kept separate.

When cool, transfer to clean, freshly lined trays and season lightly with icing sugar and salt. Reserve until ready to serve.

Garnish: Remove and discard the outer leaves of the iceberg lettuce. Carefully break away remaining inner leaves and use sharp scissors to trim them into large even-sized cups. Place in iced water to crisp.

Slice the kaffir lime leaves very finely lengthways so that you have long, hair-like strands. Bring a small pot of water to the boil and blanch them for 3 seconds then refresh in iced water. Drain and reserve until needed.

Roughly chop the roasted peanuts.

To Serve: Remove the cold chicken from the poaching liquor. Trim away and discard the wings. Carefully remove the legs and breasts and discard the remaining carcass. Gently pull away the flesh from the legs and break into smallish pieces. Slice the breasts into bite-size pieces.

Spoon a teaspoon of the chilli mayonnaise into each lettuce cup, followed by a spoonful of chicken. Next add a Vietnamese mint leaf and a pinch each of shredded kaffir lime leaf and roasted peanuts. Top with a small amount of the each of the fried Asian coleslaw ingredients, stacking them one on top of the other. Finish with a slice of crispy lotus root, season with a little extra icing sugar and salt and serve immediately.

Makes 18 cups

tea-smoked duck salad
with cucumber, chilli, lime and mandarin pancakes

Mandarin Pancakes

200 g (7 oz) plain
(all-purpose) flour

130 ml (4½ fl oz)
boiling water

2 tablespoons
peanut oil

Tea Smoked Duck

150 g (5 oz) green tea

150 g (5 oz) dark
brown sugar

200 g (7 oz)
 jasmine rice

3 duck breasts

Salad

½ cup coriander
(cilantro) leaves

½ cup mint leaves

1 long cucumber, cut
into 4 cm (1½ in) batons

2 red Lombok chillies,
finely sliced

5 spring onions
(scallions), white
part only, cut into
bite-size pieces

2 limes

50 g (2 oz) dried rice-
stick noodles

1½ tablespoons
fish sauce

1½ tablespoons
peanut oil

Dressing

2 tablespoons
hoi sin sauce

1 tablespoon
sesame oil

2 tablespoons
light soy sauce

100 ml (3½ fl oz)
cold water

juice of 1 lemon

2 red bird's eye
chillies, finely sliced

Garnish

2 tablespoons
roasted rice.
(see Basics)

Tea-smoked duck is a classic Sichuan dish, and my version sees it presented on a mandarin pancake with a refreshing salad of cucumber, ginger and coriander garnished with nutty toasted rice. The flavours are clean and intense and serve to highlight the smoky richness of the duck.

Mandarin Pancakes: Sift the flour into a basin. Bring the water to the boil, then pour onto the flour and stir well to combine. Work the dough into a ball and knead with your hands for 5–10 minutes, until it becomes smooth and elastic. Rest for 20 minutes

On a clean work surface roll the dough out into a long sausage, about 3 cm (1½ in) thick, then cut into 1.5 cm (¾ in) discs. Use a heavy rolling pin to roll each disc into a 15 cm (6 in) pancake. Brush each pancake with a little oil and stick 2 together. Roll each pair of pancakes out again to make larger 20 cm (8 in) pancakes. Continue until all the dough is used – you should end up with at least 12 pancakes. Keep them covered with a damp cloth while you work.

Heat a non-stick frying pan. Fry the pancakes in the dry pan over low heat until they start to brown in spots, then turn them over and cook the other side. Remove the pancakes from the heat, peel them apart and store, covered with a damp cloth, until ready to use.

Tea-Smoked Duck: Line a wok with kitchen foil. Mix together the tea, sugar and rice and place in the wok. Arrange the duck breasts, skin side down, on top of the mixture. Cover the wok with its lid or kitchen foil and place over a low flame until you see a little smoke emerging, about 5 minutes. Cook for a further 15 minutes, then turn off the heat and continue to smoke the duck for an hour. Remove the smoked ducks from the wok and discard the smoking mixture.

Preheat the oven to 180°C (350°F). Sear the duck breasts, skin side down, in a hot dry oven-proof frying pan until golden brown, then transfer the pan to the oven and cook for around 5–8 minutes. The duck breasts should still be pink in the centre. Allow them to rest at room temperature for a further 10 minutes before carving.

Salad: Mix together the coriander and mint leaves. Prepare the cucumber, chillies and spring onions. Peel the limes and slice the segments out of their casing.

Bring a small pot of salted water to the boil. Add the rice-stick noodles, then remove the pot from the heat and allow the noodles to soak in the hot water for 3–4 minutes, or until they are tender. Refresh under cold water, and drain thoroughly. Toss with the fish sauce and peanut oil and keep at room temperature.

Dressing: Whisk together all the dressing ingredients.

To Serve: Bring a pan of water to the boil. Place the pancakes in a lightly greased bamboo steamer basket, a few at a time, cover with the lid and steam for about a minute to warm them through.

Place the salad ingredients in a large mixing bowl. Use a very sharp knife to slice each rested breast lengthwise into about 10 thin slices. Add the duck slices to the salad. Pour over enough dressing to coat the salad lightly and toss. Divide the salad between 6 plates and drizzle a little extra dressing around the plate. Sprinkle over the roasted rice and serve with warm pancakes on the side.

Serves 6

tea-smoking

Smoking foods is another good way of imparting a different flavour dimension. For practical reasons, we use a cold-smoking technique in the restaurant and unless you have access to a special hot-smoking chamber, I recommend this for home too.

The items to be smoked are usually marinated and then placed in a closed container above the smoking mixture, which produces enough smoke to impregnate the food without cooking it. The great thing about this process is that you can cook any smoked item at a later time using any method of cooking you like. Some of the things I particularly like to smoke are duck, quail, some fish, venison and even tomatoes!

Tea-smoking is a traditional Chinese method that can be done using a hot or cold process. It is my preferred technique and one that I use all the time. The smoking mixture uses a traditional combination of tea, rice and sugar – each plays an important part. The tea (usually jasmine) burns to produce smoke. The sugar, as it burns, turns to a dark caramel that adds a nice smooth dimension to the tea. Without it, the tea itself tastes too bitter and charred. Once heated, the rice retains enough heat to keep the tea and sugar smoking.

The other fun thing about smoking is playing around with the flavours. Not only can you vary the ingredients in your spice rub or marinade, but you can also use different things in the smoking mix. For instance, I sometimes use gunpowder green tea or orange pekoe tea instead of jasmine tea in the smoking mix.

flavour balance

There is an underlying principle in South East Asian culinary traditions that involves the idea of balance. It is as fundamental to cooking as it is to the rest of life.

What that means in practical terms is that every dish needs to be balanced in temperature (hot and cold), texture (soft, slippery, crunchy) and above all flavour (sweet, salty, sour and sometimes chilli-heat). But achieving that balance is very much a question of individual preference – some people can tolerate greater amounts of chilli, for instance. Individual ingredients can vary in flavour and intensity too, depending on the season, quality and so on. It really comes down to tasting and adjusting, tasting and adjusting, until you strike the balance that feels right to you.

When it comes to quantities in my recipes, therefore, I offer them as a guide. With this style of cooking, there is no right and wrong. You just need to understand the basic principles, and take it from there.

The key flavour components, as I said before, are sweet, salty, sour and chilli-heat. And there are a variety of ingredients you can use to achieve each of these. I discuss the individual ingredients in greater detail on page 88, but in general, the sweetness will come from palm sugar, saltiness from fish sauce or soy sauce, sourness from tamarind or a citrus juice such as lime and the heat, when appropriate, comes from chilli or pepper.

Often, the flavours will be adjusted at the end of cooking the dish – particularly when making broths, soups and laksas. I always have fish sauce, lime juice and gula melaka syrup to hand so that the balance can be adjusted all the way through the cooking process, and most importantly right at the very end.

It's really a learning process, and as I say throughout this book you need to keep tasting and adjusting until the flavour balance seems right to you.

palm sugar-cured beef and chilli salad

with rice noodles, peanut praline, crispy shallots, coriander and toasted sesame oil dressing

Palm Sugar-Cured Beef	Salad	Toasted Sesame Oil Dressing	Garnish
(Needs 36 hours to cure)	50 g (1½ oz) rice-stick noodles	100 ml (3½ fl oz) peanut oil	2 teaspoons crispy shallots (see Basics)
150 g (5 oz) palm sugar, roughly chopped	1 teaspoon fish sauce	3 teaspoons sesame oil	1 teaspoon black sesame seeds
130 g (4½ oz) sea salt flakes	1 teaspoon peanut oil	2 red bird's eye chillies, finely chopped	
10 g (½ oz) Sichuan peppercorns	100 g (3½ oz) green beans, cut into halves or thirds	1 tablespoon freshly grated ginger	
5 coriander (cilantro) roots finely chopped	½ cup Vietnamese mint leaves	2 cloves garlic, finely chopped	
50 ml (1½ fl oz) light soy sauce	½ cup mint leaves	80 ml (2½ fl oz) light soy sauce	
800 g (2 lb) beef fillet, trimmed of sinews	½ cup watercress sprigs	2 teaspoons sweet soy sauce (ketjap manis)	
	½ cup pepper cress sprigs	4 teaspoons mirin	
	50 g (1½ oz) peanut praline (see Basics)	juice of 1 lemon	
	3 teaspoons candied chilli (see Basics)	1 teaspoon toasted sesame seeds	

Palm Sugar-Cured Beef: Mix together the palm sugar, sea salt, Sichuan peppercorns, chopped coriander root and soy sauce. Rub this curing mixture all over the beef fillet and place it in a shallow dish, covered with plastic wrap. Refrigerate for 36 hours, turning the beef around in the curing mix every 8 hours. Pour away the curing mix and wipe the beef clean and dry with a cloth. Sear the beef in a very hot, dry frying pan, turning so that it browns all over and caramelises. Remove from the heat, and allow to cool completely before refrigerating.

Salad: Bring two small pots of salted water to the boil. Add the rice-stick noodles to one, then remove the pot from the heat and allow the noodles to soak in the hot water for 3–4 minutes, or until they are tender. Refresh under cold water and drain thoroughly. Toss with the fish sauce and peanut oil and reserve at room temperature.

In the second pot of boiling water, blanch the beans for 2–3 minutes, then refresh in iced water, drain well and refrigerate.

Mix together the Vietnamese mint, mint leaves, watercress and pepper cress. Refrigerate until needed. Roughly chop the peanut praline and candied chilli, and refrigerate separately until ready to serve.

Toasted Sesame Oil Dressing: Heat the peanut oil and sesame oil in a frying pan and gently sauté the chilli, ginger and garlic until fragrant, 2–3 minutes. Remove from the heat and allow to cool. When cold, strain the peanut oil into a bowl and stir in the two soy sauces, mirin, lemon juice and sesame seeds. Store at room temperature until needed.

To Serve: Place all the salad ingredients in a large mixing bowl. Use a very sharp knife to carve the beef into very fine slices, and add to the salad. Pour over enough toasted sesame oil dressing to lightly coat the salad and mix everything together well.

Pile a generous mound of salad on each plate. Drizzle extra dressing around the salad and top with a pinch of crispy shallots and a sprinkle of black sesame seeds.

Serves 6

hot and sour thai beef salad
with roasted rice

Marinated Beef

(Marinate overnight)

80 ml (2½ fl oz)
sweet soy sauce
(ketjap manis)

2 tablespoons
grated ginger

3 cloves garlic,
finely chopped garlic

800 g (28 oz) beef
scotch fillet, trimmed
of all fat and sinews

**Hot and Sour
Dressing**

100 ml (3½ fl oz)
lime juice

40 ml (1¼ fl oz)
fish sauce

2 red bird's eye
chillies, finely chopped

2 green bird's eye
chillies, finely chopped

4 teaspoons gula
melaka syrup
(see Basics)

Salad

1 long cucumber,
cut into 4 cm
(1½ in) batons

1 medium red
onion, finely sliced

100 g (3½ oz) green
beans, blanched

1½ cups fresh
coriander (cilantro)
leaves

1½ cups fresh
mint leaves

1 cup watercress sprigs

3 tablespoons ginger,
cut into julienne strips

1 red Lombok chilli,
cut into julienne strips

4 fresh kaffir lime
leaves, finely shredded

1 lemongrass stalk,
white part only,
finely chopped

2 tablespoons
roasted rice
(see Basics)

There must be hundreds of versions of this Thai classic dish. Mine includes some nutty, crunchy roasted rice as well as the vital flavours of coriander, mint and spring onions. The dressing is big and bold – but that's the way it should be.

Marinated Beef: Mix together the sweet soy sauce, ginger and garlic and rub all over the beef. Place in the refrigerator and marinate overnight.

Preheat the oven to 180°C (350°F). Wipe the beef dry and sear in a very hot, dry frying pan until it is brown and caramelised all over. Place the beef in the oven and cook for around 10 minutes for medium-rare. Allow to cool completely, then slice finely.

Hot and Sour Dressing: Mix together the lime juice, fish sauce and chillies. Leave to stand for 5 minutes. Taste to check the balance of flavours, and adjust with a little extra lime juice or fish sauce if necessary. Stir in the gula melaka.

Salad: Place the beef slices in a large bowl. Pour on the hot and sour dressing and leave to macerate for 2 minutes. In a separate bowl, mix together the cucumber, onion, green beans, fresh herbs, ginger, chilli, lime leaves and lemongrass.

To serve: Add the salad to the macerated beef and toss to combine. Divide between 6 plates and sprinkle generously with the roasted rice. Drizzle a little extra dressing round each plate before serving.

Serves 6

whitelaw cheese and fig salad

with fine herbs, rockmelon, prosciutto and balsamic syrup

Whitelaw Cheese Salad

250 g (9 oz) Whitelaw cheese, at room temperature

1 tablespoon cream cheese, at room temperature

1 tablespoon chervil

1 tablespoon dill

1 tablespoon chives

salt and pepper

6 ripe black figs

Garnish

¼ rockmelon

6 very fine slices prosciutto

1 tablespoon brown sugar

12 mint leaves

balsamic syrup (see Basics)

Whitelaw Cheese Salad: Drain both cheeses well and place in a large bowl. Roughly chop the chervil and dill (if they are too fine they will lose texture and flavour). Chop the chives finely, combine with other herbs and reserve. Add the herbs to the cheeses and mix together gently until well combined. Season with salt and pepper.

Using a sharp knife, trim the tops and bottoms from the figs, peel them as carefully as possible and reserve.

Garnish: Halve the rockmelon crosswise, remove the peel and discard the seeds. Using a sharp knife, slice the rockmelon lengthways into 2-mm slices, then cut each slice into bite-size pieces, no larger than the figs.

Preheat oven to 200ºC (400ºF). Cut each slice of prosciutto in half, lay on a very lightly oiled baking tray and sprinkle lightly with the brown sugar. Place in oven and cook for around 3–4 minutes, until the prosciutto is crisp and the sugar has caramelised. Watch carefully to ensure the sugar doesn't burn and become bitter.

To Serve: Slice each fig in half and place two halves on each plate. Top each fig with a piece of rockmelon and a mint leaf followed by a small scoop of the herbed cheese. To finish, stick a piece of caramelised prosciutto into the cheese and drizzle a little balsamic syrup around the plate in a neat spiral.

Note: Any good quality fresh curd cheese will work well in this dish. Alternatively, blend together two parts of sheep's milk ricotta and one part mascarpone.

Serves 6

fried sheep's milk fetta

with roasted pear and rocket salad, pomegranate molasses and cinnamon sugar

Fried Fetta

600 g (1¼ lb)
block of firm sheep's
milk fetta

100 g (3½ oz) plain
(all-purpose) flour

100 ml (3½ fl oz)
egg wash (see Basics)

200 g (7 oz) fresh
breadcrumbs

100 ml (3½ fl oz)
clarified butter
or ghee

Roasted Pear
and Rocket Salad

2 ripe pears

1 tablespoon clarified
butter or ghee

2 cups baby rocket

1 teaspoon olive oil

salt and pepper

Dressing

50 ml (1½ fl oz)
pomegranate molasses

40 ml (2½ fl oz)
olive oil

juice of ½ small lemon

Cinnamon Sugar

1 teaspoon
ground cinnamon

1½ teaspoons
icing (confectioners')
sugar

I presented this dish at the Melbourne Masterclass in 1997. It has all the flavour and texture combinations I love in food – I particularly like the idea of serving sweet cinnamon sugar with salty fetta. The sour-sweetness of pomegranate molasses lifts the dish to another dimension. It is very simple to prepare, but is packed with flavour.

Fried Fetta: Using a sharp knife, slice the fetta into 6 slices, about 10 cm x 10 cm (4 in x 4 in). It may help to dip the knife into hot water from time to time, which will make slicing easier and neater. Cut each slice in half diagonally to form two triangles, and then cut each of these large triangles in half. You will now have 4 bite-size fetta triangles per person. Lightly dust the fetta triangles in flour, shaking off any excess; be careful not to break the fetta. Dip the cheese into the egg wash and then the breadcrumbs. Repeat this dipping and crumbing twice more, so you have a good thick crumb coating. This is important, as you need a good crisp crust to contain the molten cheese while it is frying. Lay the slices on a tray, cover and refrigerate until ready to fry.

Roasted Pear and Rocket Salad: Peel and halve the pears and remove the core and stem. Cut each half into 4 thick slices. Heat the clarified butter or ghee in a large frying pan until it starts to bubble. Sauté the pear slices until golden brown. Make sure they do not overcook and remain firm to the touch.

Dressing: Stir together the pomegranate molasses, olive oil and lemon juice and keep until needed.

Cinnamon Sugar: Mix together the cinnamon and icing sugar and keep in a dry place ready for dusting.

To Serve: Heat the 100 ml clarified butter or ghee in a large frying pan until it bubbles. Fry the cheese slices, 4 at a time, until golden brown, about 2 minutes. Carefully turn and brown on the other side for another minute, then remove from the pan and drain on absorbent paper. Keep warm while you fry the remaining cheese slices.

In a large bowl carefully mix the pear and rocket together, dress lightly with the oil and season to taste.

Place a small mound of the salad in the centre of each plate. Neatly stack 4 fetta triangles on top and drizzle a little extra dressing around the plate. Use a tea-strainer or sugar-shaker and dust lightly with cinnamon sugar.

Serves 6 as a generous starter

smoky eggplant, artichoke and tomato salad

with sumac-spiced yoghurt cheese, herb salad and pomegranate molasses

Smoky Eggplant, Artichoke and Tomato Salad

3 cooked globe artichokes (see Basics)

1 medium eggplant (aubergine)

2 vine-ripened tomatoes

1 red onion, finely sliced

½ bunch chives, cut into 4 cm (1½ in) lengths

1 lemon

salt

freshly ground black pepper

Yoghurt Cheese

200 g (7 oz) labna (see Basics)

½ cup sumac

Dressing

2 teaspoons lemon juice

1 teaspoon extra-virgin olive oil

salt and pepper

Garnish

1 sourdough roll (or another sturdy white-bread roll)

2 tablespoons extra-virgin olive oil

½ cup fresh dill

½ cup fresh chervil

½ cup fresh chives

3 tablespoons pomegranate molasses

3 tablespoons extra-virgin olive oil

This dish represents something of a culture clash – the Middle East comes to Italy, perhaps! Pomegranate molasses is a luscious syrup from the Middle East, both sweet and tangy. It really brings out the vibrant flavours of the artichokes, eggplant and vine-ripened tomatoes.

Smoky Eggplant, Artichoke and Tomato Salad: Cook the artichokes according to the Basic recipe. Peel the leaves from the artichoke and reserve. Cut the hearts into quarters and reserve.

Prick the eggplant all over with a fork and wrap tightly in 2 layers of kitchen foil. Sit the eggplant directly on a high flame on your stove, or place on a barbecue. Cook for about 2 minutes until steam begins to rise from the foil. (The eggplant should be just tender, not collapsed and mushy). Use tongs to remove the eggplant from the heat, place it in a bowl and allow it to cool. When cool, remove the foil and carefully peel away the skin. Slice the eggplant into quarters. If there are any seeds, slice them away and slice each quarter into long strips. Reserve until needed.

Bring a small pot of water to the boil and blanch the tomatoes for around 10 seconds. Refresh in iced water for a further 10 seconds and carefully peel away the skin. Cut each tomato into quarters and gently squeeze out the seeds. Slice each quarter into strips and reserve until needed.

Peel the lemon and carefully remove each segment from the pith. Dice and reserve.

Sumac-Spiced Yoghurt Cheese: Roll the labna into 6 balls and coat in sumac.

Garnish: Preheat the grill. Cut the sourdough roll into 6 slices, around 5–8 mm (¼–½ in) thick. and lightly brush on both sides with olive oil. Toast each piece under the grill, then store in a dry place until needed.

Combine the herbs and refrigerate until needed.

To Serve: In a large bowl mix together the artichoke leaves and hearts, the diced lemon, eggplant, tomato, red onion and chives. Season with salt and freshly ground black pepper. Whisk together the lemon juice, olive oil, salt and pepper and lightly dress the salad.

Place a neat mound of salad in the centre of each plate and top with a toasted sourdough crouton and a ball of labna. Finish off with a small handful of the fresh herbs and drizzle the plate with a little pomegranate molasses and olive oil.

Serves 6

chargrilled asparagus
with gippsland blue cheese bavarois, nut oil dressing and garlic nougatine

Garlic Oil

½ head of garlic

250 ml (9 fl oz) olive oil

Garlic Nougatine

125 g (4½ oz) flaked almonds

165 g (5½ oz) caster (superfine) sugar

2 tablespoons garlic oil

Blue Cheese Bavarois

125 g (4½ oz) soft blue cheese

250 ml (9 fl oz) milk

3 egg yolks

3 gelatine leaves

30 ml (1 fl oz) hot water

250 ml (9 fl oz) thickened cream

1 tablespoon chopped chives

salt

freshly ground black pepper

Nut Oil Dressing

50 ml (1½ fl oz) hazelnut oil

1½ tablespoons walnut oil

1½ tablespoons cabernet vinegar

1 teaspoon Dijon mustard

2 shallots, finely chopped

salt

freshly ground black pepper

Chargrilled Asparagus

500 g (1 lb) thin asparagus spears

2 tablespoons olive oil

juice of ½ lemon

salt

pepper

Garlic Oil: Wrap the garlic in a tea towel and bruise it lightly with a rolling pin or the base of a heavy kitchen knife. Place the garlic in a small saucepan with the olive oil. Heat gently until lukewarm, then turn off the heat and leave to infuse for at least 20 minutes.

Garlic Nougatine: Toast the almonds in a dry pan until they are lightly and evenly coloured, then grind to a fine powder. Place the sugar in a saucepan and cook over a medium heat until the sugar dissolves and turns to a light golden caramel. Stir in the ground almonds, cook gently for another minute then add the garlic oil.

While the mixture is still warm, tip it out onto a sheet of greaseproof paper. Lay another sheet of greaseproof paper on top and use a rolling pin to roll the nougatine out to 2 mm (⅛ in) thickness. Peel away the top sheet of paper and cut the nougatine into small triangles while it is still pliable. The nougatine can be made ahead of time and stored in an airtight container for several days. If made ahead of time, the nougatine should be flashed in the microwave for 10 seconds before using to make it pliable.

Blue Cheese Bavarois: Pass the blue cheese through a fine sieve and put into a saucepan with the milk. Bring to a gentle simmer, stirring constantly until the cheese melts. Be careful not to let the mixture boil. Whisk the egg yolks in a large bowl. Strain the hot milk onto the eggs and whisk well. Return the custard to the saucepan and cook gently until the mixture thickens enough to coat the back of a spoon.

Meanwhile, soak the gelatine in cold water for about a minute until it softens, then squeeze out any excess water. Stir the gelatine in the hot water until it dissolves completely, and add to the cooked custard. Stir well then pour the custard through a fine sieve into a clean bowl and place in a sink of iced water to chill.

Whip the cream until it forms soft peaks. When the custard is cold and is on the verge of setting, fold in the whipped cream. Stir through the chives and season with salt and pepper to taste. Ladle the mixture into 6 oiled dariole moulds and refrigerate until set.

Nut Oil Dressing: Stir all the ingredients together and taste. Adjust seasonings if necessary and store at room temperature.

To Serve: Snap the woody ends off the asparagus and peel about two-thirds of the way along each stalk. Wash and dry the asparagus and roll in the olive oil and lemon juice. Season with salt and pepper.

Preheat a griddle plate or barbecue to its hottest setting. Cook the asparagus until tender, turning frequently.

To serve, carefully unmould a bavarois onto each bowl. Arrange the asparagus spears around the bavarois, drizzle with nut oil dressing and serve garnished with a triangle of garlic nougatine.

Serves 6

mains

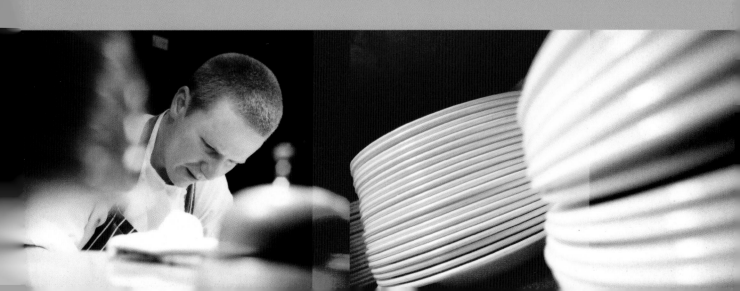

baby snapper with roasted rice crust
with cucumber, coriander, shaved coconut salad and red nam jim

Red Nam Jim

10 red Lombok chillies, seeded and roughly chopped

1 red bird's eye chilli, seeded and roughly chopped

2 cloves garlic, roughly chopped

3 coriander (cilantro) roots, roughly chopped

50 g (2 oz) grated palm sugar

250 ml (9 fl oz) lime juice

60 ml (2 fl oz) fish sauce

Cucumber, Coriander and Shaved Coconut Salad

1 small coconut

1 long cucumber

1 red onion

1 cup coriander (cilantro) leaves

1 cup mint leaves

6 fresh kaffir lime leaves, finely shredded

Snapper

6 x 150 g (5 oz) snapper fillets, pin bones removed

100 g (3½ oz) roasted rice (see Basics)

freshly ground sea salt

125 ml (4 fl oz) olive oil

Garnish

crispy shallots (see Basics)

300 g (10 oz) steamed jasmine rice (see Basics)

Red Nam Jim: Place all the roughly chopped chillies in a mortar with the garlic and coriander roots and pound to a fine paste. Add the palm sugar and lime juice, a little at a time, and continue to pound until it is all incorporated. Add the fish sauce, a little at a time, until you achieve a good balance of sweet, sour and salty. Reserve until ready to use.

Cucumber, Coriander and Shaved Coconut Salad: Use a hammer to crack the coconut open. Use a small sharp knife or screwdriver to prise the coconut flesh away from the hard outer shell – there will still be a layer of dark skin attached. Cut the coconut into pieces and place on a naked flame, skin-side down. Toast for 3–4 minutes, moving the coconut pieces constantly to make sure they don't burn. Allow to cool, and use a vegetable peeler or sharp knife to slice the coconut into long thin shavings and reserve.

Peel the cucumber and use a vegetable peeler or sharp knife to slice into long shavings. Finely slice the onion crosswise, into thin rings. Prepare the remaining ingredients and keep until ready to serve.

To Serve: Preheat the oven to 180ºC (350ºF). Lightly dust the snapper with roasted rice so you have a thin even coating, and season with freshly ground sea salt. Heat a teaspoon of olive oil in a large non-stick pan and fry the snapper fillets, skin side down, for 3–4 minutes. Do not move them about in the pan and they will develop a crispy golden coating with a good nutty flavour. Place the snapper fillets in the hot oven and cook for a further 1–2 minutes, or until the flesh is just cooked. Carefully remove them from the oven and drain on absorbent paper.

In a large mixing bowl, combine the salad ingredients. Place a small mound of salad on each plate and drizzle with red nam jim. Arrange a snapper fillet on top of the salad and garnish with crispy fried shallots. Serve with steamed jasmine rice.

Note: When purchasing snapper fillets, request that they are long-line caught rather than trawled, as the quality is much better.

Serves 6

tempura-fried fish and chips
with lime, soy and sesame salt

Crispy Fried Garnish

1 litre (1¾ pints) peanut oil for frying

1 taro

1 fresh lotus root

½ teaspoon icing (confectioners') sugar

½ teaspoon sea salt, lightly ground

Sweet Soy Dressing

100 ml (3 fl oz) sweet soy sauce (ketjap manis)

50 ml (1½ fl oz) light soy sauce

50 ml (1½ fl oz) Japanese soy sauce (tamari)

Sesame Salt

2 tablespoons sesame seeds

2 tablespoons sea salt

Tempura-fried Fish

6 large flathead fillets, 150 g (5 oz) each, skin and bones removed

1 cup plain (all-purpose) flour

300 ml (10½ fl oz) chilled tempura batter (see Basics)

Garnish

6 teaspoons sesame salt

3 limes

This is my version of fish and chips – with a distinctly Asian feel to it. It is a very popular lunchtime dish at the restaurant, as everyone loves the combination of piping-hot crispy fish with its dressing of tangy lime, soy and nutty sesame. The crispy fried vegetables make a very pleasant change from the more traditional chips, but if you are unable to find fresh lotus root then omit it from the dish; frozen lotus root will not do.

Crispy Fried Garnish: Preheat the peanut oil. Peel the taro and the lotus root. Use a binriner slicer or a very sharp knife to slice the taro as finely as possible, then cut into fine julienne strips. Slice the lotus root finely on a 45° angle. Sprinkle the shredded taro onto the hot oil in small batches and fry for 1–2 minutes, until it turns crispy. Drain on absorbent paper and allow to cool, then sprinkle with the icing sugar and salt. Fry the lotus root in small batches until it turns golden brown and crispy. Drain on absorbent paper and allow to cool, then sprinkle with the icing sugar and salt. Store the vegetables separately in a dry place until ready to use. Reserve the oil for frying the fish.

Sweet Soy Dressing: Whisk the three soy sauces together and keep until needed.

Sesame Salt: Preheat oven to 200°C (400°F). Plase sesame seeds on an oven tray and toast in hot oven for 2–3 minutes or until golden brown. Remove and cool. Grind the sesame seeds and salt together using a mortar and pestle.

To Serve: Heat the peanut oil to 180°C (350°F). Slice each flathead fillet lengthways into long fingers. You should get about 2–3 fingers from an average-sized fillet. Dust each finger of flathead lightly with flour, shaking off any excess. Dip into the tempura batter and deep-fry, two at a time, for 3–4 minutes, until crispy and golden brown. Drain on absorbent paper and sprinkle the hot fish with a little sesame salt.

Arrange the long fingers of fish in the centre of each plate and top with a mound of crispy fried taro. Finish with a slice of crispy lotus root. Serve with halves of lime and little dishes of sesame salt and sweet soy dressing.

Note: A very attractive way of presenting this dish is the way we do it in the restaurant. On each large white plate lay a square of Chinese newspaper, topped with a square of banana leaf – each about 13 x 13 cm (5 x 5 in). Arrange the fish and crispy taro on top of the banana leaf. Next to the fish place little individual dishes of sesame salt and sweet soy dressing. Wrap each lime half in a small square of muslin, tied into a neat tight knot to trap the pips as you squeeze, add to the plate and serve.

Serves 6

flavours

Although the look and texture of food is important, to me good cooking is mainly all about maximising flavour. It is something that I have learnt through my fascination with foods from South East Asia, where every type of aromatic herb and spice is used to excite the palate.

Typically, many different herbs and spices are blended to achieve something that is far greater than the sum of its individual components, and as I say time and time again, it is all about achieving balance. Here are some of the typical flavour components that I like to use in my cooking:

sweet

The sweet element of a dish usually comes from palm sugar. If you visit an Asian grocer you'll discover that this comes in a variety of shapes, sizes and colours, which can be quite confusing. As a rule of thumb, darker palm sugars tend to have a stronger flavour than lighter ones as they are less refined. Don't worry about the shape – the semi-circular palm sugar gets its shape because it is traditionally set in coconut shells. Similarly the little logs of sugar are traditionally set in bamboo.

I prefer to use a dark palm sugar from Thailand, and I nearly always boil it into a dark sugar syrup called gula melaka for ease of use (see recipe in Basics, page 7). Gula melaka can also be flavoured with other aromatics like mandarin peel, cinnamon or allspice. It is incredibly versatile and useful for sweet and savoury dishes.

salty

Usually, saltiness comes from fish sauce, shrimp paste and soy sauce. I also use two traditional Japanese ingredients, bonito (dried fish flakes) and dashi (dried seaweed).

When it comes to soy sauce, I am quite discerning. I tend to avoid most Chinese soy sauces as they are made from hydrolysed soy protein (the soy beans are boiled with hydrochloric acid to accelerate the fermentation process). To my palate their flavour is coarse and overly salty.

I use three different types of soy sauce in my cooking. I use tamari, which is a light, aromatic Japanese soy sauce; Taiwanese soy sauce, which has a refined yet slightly fuller flavour; and ketjap manis, a thick, sweet soy sauce from Indonesia.

sour

Citrus juices are most commonly used throughout South East Asia to add the essential sour component to a dish. Lime is popular, but I also use lemons, grapefruit, oranges, soursops and pomelos.

Tamarind is the most widely used ingredient to achieve a sour flavour.

A more subtle sourness can be achieved through using kaffir lime leaves, lemongrass and also dried citrus peels. They each add their own distinctive floral or aromatic note.

hot

Usually, heat comes from fresh and dried chillies, Sichuan pepper, wasabi, black pepper and even fresh ginger. All of these can vary in intensity, so always taste them before adding to a dish. I tend to use a combination of small, hot red bird's eye chillies, and longer, milder red and green Lombok chillies.

coconut fried garfish

with vietnamese rice noodle salad and hot tamarind dressing

Hot Tamarind Dressing

150 g (5 oz) seedless tamarind paste

125 ml (4 fl oz) Japanese rice wine vinegar

300 ml (10½ fl oz) water

150 g (5 oz) white sugar

2 cloves garlic

40 g (1½ oz) fresh ginger, peeled

2 stalks lemongrass, white part only

4 red bird's eye chillies, roughly chopped

4 fresh kaffir lime leaves, roughly chopped

1 bunch coriander (cilantro), roughly chopped

50 ml (1½ fl oz) lime juice

Vietnamese Rice Noodle Salad

100 g (3½ oz) rice-stick noodles

1 tablespoon peanut oil

50 ml (1½ fl oz) fish sauce

100 g (3½ oz) raw cashew nuts

100 g (3½ oz) green beans, blanched

2 pink grapefruit, segments removed from skin

½ head iceberg lettuce, finely shredded

1 cup Vietnamese mint leaves, roughly chopped

1 cup coriander (cilantro) leaves, roughly chopped

½ cup pickled green papaya (see Basics)

2 teaspoons pickled ginger (see Basics), cut into julienne strips

2 teaspoons crispy shallot garnish (see Basics)

juice of 1 lime

Garnish

3 limes

Coconut Batter

70 g (3 oz) plain (all-purpose) flour

35 g (1½ oz) powdered coconut milk

1 egg

250 ml (9 fl oz) coconut milk

Garfish

6 x 130 g (4½ oz) garfish, cleaned and filleted into butterflies, so that the two halves remain attached to each other

200 ml (7 fl oz) clarified butter

100 g (3½ oz) plain (all-purpose) flour

This is one of my all-time favourite dishes, with a unique combination of flavours. It is quite a challenging dish to prepare – the batter is not crispy, but moist and delicate – however it is worth mastering.

Hot Tamarind Dressing: Soak the tamarind paste in enough warm water to just cover it. Let stand in a warm place for 10 minutes to soften. Work with your hands for 2–3 minutes to form a paste, then push it through a sieve to remove any seeds.

Put the rice wine vinegar, water and sugar in a non-reactive saucepan and simmer until the sugar dissolves.

Use a rolling pin or the heavy end of a cook's knife to bruise the garlic, ginger and lemongrass and add them to the syrup. Add the remaining ingredients (except the lime juice) and simmer very gently for 20 minutes. Remove from the heat and allow the flavours to infuse for another 20 minutes before straining. Allow the dressing to cool, then stir in the lime juice. This dressing should be light and intensely flavoured: a nice balance of sour, sweet and hot.

Vietnamese Rice Noodle Salad: Bring a small pot of water to the boil. Add the rice-stick noodles, then remove the pot from the heat and allow the noodles to soak in the hot water for 3–4 minutes, or until they are tender. Refresh under cold water, then drain thoroughly. Tip the noodles into a mixing bowl and stir through the peanut oil and half the fish sauce. Keep at room temperature until ready to serve.

Preheat the oven to 170ºC (325ºF). Roast the cashew nuts until golden brown, shaking the baking tray every couple of minutes so they colour evenly.

Prepare the remaining salad ingredients and store separately until ready to serve.

Garnish: Cut a muslin cloth into 6 squares, 10 cm x 10 cm (4 in x 4 in). Cut the limes in half and place one half, cut side down, in the centre of each muslin square. Bring the four corners of each square together and tie tightly into a neat knot. Refrigerate until ready to serve.

Coconut Batter: Sift the flour and coconut milk powder into a bowl. Beat in the egg and slowly whisk in the coconut milk to form a thick batter. Make sure it is free of lumps and use it as soon as possible, it does not keep well.

To Serve: Preheat the oven to 200ºC (400ºF). When ready to cook the garfish, heat the clarified butter in a large non-stick ovenproof frying pan until it starts to bubble. Cook the garfish one at a time. Hold the fish by its head and tail and dip in flour, shaking off any excess. Dip lightly in the coconut batter, draining off any excess. Fry skin-side down until golden, 2–3 minutes. Turn the fish over, transfer to an oven tray. Repeat for all 6 garfish. Place oven trays with garfish into the oven and cook for 2–3 minutes or until warmed through. Drain on absorbent paper before serving.

Put all the salad ingredients in a large bowl and mix together with the lime juice and the rest of the fish sauce.

Place a generous mound of salad on each serving plate. Arrange the garfish on top and pour over a generous amount of tamarind dressing. Garnish with the muslin-wrapped lime and serve straight away.

Serves 6

soy-glazed snapper

with avocado, mango and pink grapefruit, candied chillies, crispy shallots and lime-syrup dressing

Soy Glaze

50 g (2 oz) honey

75 ml (3 fl oz) sweet soy sauce (ketjap manis)

100 ml (3½ fl oz) light soy sauce

Lime-Syrup Dressing

400 g (14 oz) palm sugar, roughly chopped

400 ml 14 fl oz) water

1 long red chilli, seeded and finely sliced

1 long green chilli, seeded and finely sliced

zest and juice of 3 limes

Salad

1 large pink grapefruit

1 large mango

1 large avocado

100 g candied chilli (see Basics)

¼ cup Vietnamese mint leaves

Snapper

100 ml (3½ fl oz) olive oil

6 x 160 g (5½ oz) snapper fillets, pin bones removed

sea salt

Garnish

½ cup crispy shallots (see Basics)

This dish has great contrasting flavours. The sticky sweet soy and lime-syrup dressing is a refreshing combination. A great summer dish.

Soy Glaze: Heat the honey, ketjap manis and light soy sauce in a shallow saucepan. Simmer until it just starts to smoke. Watch very carefully and remove from the heat as soon as it darkens and begins to caramelise (be careful not to let it burn). As it cools, the glaze will become sticky and jam-like. Tip into a small container and reserve.

Lime-Syrup Dressing: Place the palm sugar in a large heavy-based saucepan. Add the water, bring to the boil and simmer for around 10 minutes to form a light caramel. Brush down the inside of the pan with cold water from time to time to stop it from crystallising. When the syrup is just starting to colour, remove it from the heat and allow to cool slightly. Add the sliced red and green chillies, lime zest and juice and stir well.

Salad: Peel the pink grapefruit and use a sharp knife to slice out each segment from its casing.

Slice off each mango 'cheek' and use a large spoon to carefully scoop out the flesh. Cut into 1 cm (½ in) dice and reserve. Slice the avocado in half lengthwise, remove the stone and carefully scoop out the flesh. Cut into 1 cm (½ in) dice and reserve.

Prepare the remaining salad ingredients and keep separately until ready to serve.

To Serve: Preheat the oven to 200ºC (400ºF). When ready to cook the snapper, heat the oil in an ovenproof frying pan. Season the snapper fillets with salt and cook, skin-side down, for 2–3 minutes. Pour the soy glaze over the fish and transfer the pan to the oven. Cook for around 2 minutes, or until the snapper is just cooked.

Mix the salad ingredients together and place a generous amount on each plate. Top with a snapper fillet and a pinch of crispy shallots. Drizzle the lime-syrup dressing around the plate and serve straight away.

Serves 6

crispy garnishes

Crispy garnishes of shredded vegetables or noodles are a key part of my cooking. As I've said time and again in this book, one of the most important things about cooking is to create balance in a dish. And balance in textures is just as important as balancing flavours.

I love to use crispy garnishes, because in my view they provide that final touch to a dish. Not only do they add height and drama, but they are a really good way to introduce a crunchy note to a dish.

Typically, I use vegetables such as carrot, onions, leeks or taro. The vegetables should be shredded as finely as possible, into hair-like strands. They are then sprinkled into the hot oil in small pinches, and they will turn golden brown in just a few seconds. (Remember that onions always look a little soggy when they are removed from the oil to drain. But don't worry, they crisp up as they cool down.)

The final critical stage is to season the fried vegetables. This is a trick I learnt while visiting the kitchens of a Chinese restaurant in Hong Kong. Straight from the oil deep-fried vegetables are rather bland and flavourless, but if you season them with a little salt and sugar they spring to life.

roasted barramundi

with a red salad of baby beets, grapefruit, radicchio, capers and marinated goat's fetta and fresh herb dressing

Red Salad

2 bunches
baby beetroots

1 tablespoon extra-virgin olive oil

1 tablespoon
balsamic vinegar

1 teaspoon fresh
thyme, roughly
chopped

1 teaspoon dark
brown sugar

1 large pink
grapefruit,
segmented

1 large red onion,
halved and finely
sliced lengthwise

1½ tablespoons
baby salted capers,
very well rinsed

1 radicchio lettuce,
red leaves only,
roughly shredded

120 g (4 oz)
marinated goat's
fetta, chilled

20 ml (¾ fl oz) extra-virgin olive oil

sea salt

freshly ground
black pepper

Fresh Herb Dressing

½ cup parsley leaves

¼ cup mint leaves

¼ cup basil leaves

1 teaspoon baby salted
capers, very well rinsed

150 ml (5 fl oz) extra-virgin olive oil

sea salt

freshly ground
black pepper

Barramundi

6 x 160 g (5½ oz)
barramundi fillets

80 ml (2½ fl oz)
pure olive oil

sea salt

This is a great dish for late autumn-early winter, as it uses ingredients that are at their best then. It is a good example of combining hot and cold components in the one dish – the tangy red salad works beautifully with a simply roasted piece of white fish.

Red Salad: Preheat the oven to 180ºC (350ºF). Trim the leaves and stems away from the beetroot, leaving about 2.5 cm (1 in) attached. If you trim them too close to the roots, a lot of the colour will leach away as they cook. Wash the beetroots very well, making sure there is no dirt or grit still lurking in the stems. Mix the beetroots with the olive oil, balsamic vinegar, thyme and brown sugar then tip into a small deep baking dish and roast for about 20 minutes, until they are tender and caramelised.

Allow the beetroots to cool, cut them into halves. Prepare the remaining salad ingredients and reserve until just ready to serve.

Fresh Herb Dressing: Make sure the herb leaves are thoroughly dry. Place in a food processor with the capers and olive oil and blitz to a smooth purée. Taste and season with pepper and salt, if needed.

To Serve: Preheat the oven to 200ºC (400ºF). Brush a little oil on the barramundi fillets and sprinkle them with sea salt. Heat the remaining oil in a large ovenproof frying pan until hot. Fry the barramundi fillets, skin side down, for 2–3 minutes until nicely brown, then place in the oven for 4–5 minutes. When the fillets are cooked right through, remove them from the oven. Turn them over and allow them to rest in the pan for 2–3 minutes before draining on absorbent paper.

Place all the salad ingredients in a large mixing bowl, add the olive oil, season lightly and toss until well combined. Arrange a mound of salad on each plate and top with a barramundi fillet. Drizzle with the herb dressing and serve straight away so the cheese doesn't melt.

Serves 6

roasted blue eye

with hummus, mint yoghurt, cumin salt, lemon, pomegranate and a crispy onion salad

Mint Yoghurt

(Requires 24 hours)

350 g (12 oz)
plain yoghurt

½ cup mint leaves

½ cup flat-leaf parsley

sea salt

Hummus

100 g (3½ oz)
chickpeas, soaked
overnight in twice
their volume of water

2 tablespoons
tahini paste

3 cloves garlic,
crushed

juice of 2
medium lemons

2 tablespoons
hot water

sea salt

freshly ground
black pepper

Cumin Salt

1 tablespoon
cumin seeds

2 tablespoons
sea salt

Crispy Onion Salad

1 litre (1¾ pints)
vegetable oil

2 medium brown
onions, sliced into
fine rings

1 teaspoon sea salt

1 teaspoon icing
(confectioners') sugar

½ cup mint leaves

½ cup dill

½ cup flat-leaf
parsley leaves

Blue Eye

6 x 150 g (5 oz)
blue eye fillets,
skin removed

30 ml (1 fl oz)
olive oil

sea salt

freshly ground
black pepper

Garnish

100 ml (3½ fl oz)
pomegranate
molasses

2 lemons,
segmented

Mint Yoghurt: Rinse a square of muslin or cheesecloth under cold running water, then squeeze it dry. While the cloth is still damp, spoon 300 g (10 oz) of the yoghurt into the centre, bring together the corners and tie with twine. Suspend this hanging-bag over a deep bowl and put in the refrigerator to drain for 24 hours.

Put the herbs into a food processor with the remaining 50 g (2 oz) of yoghurt. Blitz to a fine purée. Tip the hung yoghurt into a large bowl and stir in the yoghurt-herb purée. Season with salt to taste and refrigerate.

Hummus: Rinse the soaked chickpeas thoroughly then place in a large saucepan of fresh water and bring to the boil. Lower the heat, cover the pan and cook for 20–30 minutes, or until tender. Drain off the water and let the chickpeas steam dry for a few minutes. Place the tahini paste in a food processor and blitz until it just begins to thicken. Add the garlic and lemon juice and purée until smooth. With the motor running, add 2 tablespoons hot water and then the warm chickpeas. Blitz to a very smooth purée, then taste and adjust the seasoning until you get the right balance of acidic lemon and pungent garlic.

Cumin Salt: Heat a small frying pan, add the cumin seeds and sea salt and dry fry until fragrant, about 2–3 minutes. Toss from time to time, to make sure the cumin seeds don't burn. Remove from the heat and allow to cool, then use a mortar and pestle to grind to a fine powder.

Crispy Onion Salad: Heat the vegetable oil in a small saucepan to 160ºC (350ºF). Fry the onions in several small batches until deep brown. Remove with a slotted spoon and drain on absorbent paper. Season with salt and sugar and store in a dry place until needed. Don't worry if the onions seem soft. They will crisp up as they cool down.

To Serve: Preheat the oven to 200ºC (400ºF). To cook the blue eye, heat the olive oil in a large ovenproof frying pan. Season the fish fillets with salt and pepper and fry for 1–2 minutes to colour. Transfer to the oven and cook for a further 5–10 minutes. Allow to rest on absorbent paper for a minute before serving.

Spoon a generous amount of hummus onto the middle of each plate and drizzle the pomegranate molasses around the outside. Place a portion of blue eye on top of the hummus and spoon over the mint yoghurt. Mix together the crispy onions and fresh herbs and place a small handful on top of each piece of blue eye. Sprinkle with cumin salt and lemon segments and serve.

Serves 6

roasted barramundi
with yellow curry dressing and baby shoot salad

Curry Paste

10 candlenuts,
lightly roasted

2 tablespoons shrimp
paste, lightly roasted

1 tablespoon coriander
seeds, roasted

10 red shallots, peeled

40 g (1½ oz) fresh
ginger, peeled and
roughly chopped

30 g (1 oz) fresh
galangal, peeled and
roughly chopped

40 g (1½ oz) fresh
turmeric, peeled

5 fresh kaffir lime leaves

5 cloves garlic

5 coriander roots

3 red bird's eye chillies

Yellow Curry Dressing

1 tablespoon peanut oil

800 ml (1½ pints)
coconut milk

2 tablespoons tamarind
paste (see Basics)

30 ml (1 fl oz) lime juice

1½ tablespoons
fish sauce

1½ tablespoons
gula melaka syrup
(see Basics)

Baby Shoot Salad

½ cup coriander leaves

1 cup mixed baby
Asian cresses

1 cup snow
pea shoots

Garnish

2 bunches
Chinese broccoli

2 tablespoons
peanut oil

300 g (10½ oz)
steamed jasmine
rice (see Basics)

Barramundi

6 x 160 g (5½ oz)
barramundi fillets

ground sea salt

olive oil for pan-frying

Curry Paste: Place all the ingredients in a mortar and pestle or food processor and grind to a fine paste.

Yellow Curry Dressing: Heat the peanut oil in a saucepan then add the curry paste and cook for about 10 minutes until fragrant. Add the coconut milk and bring to a simmer. Remove from the heat and leave it to cool down. Push the dressing through a sieve to extract as much flavour as possible, then discard the spice paste. Season the dressing with tamarind, lime juice, fish sauce and gula melaka to taste.

Baby Shoot Salad: Gently combine all the ingredients and reserve until ready to serve.

To Serve: To prepare the Chinese broccoli, remove the leaves from the stalks, tear them into bite-sized pieces and reserve. Cut the stalks into bite-sized pieces and blanch for 10 seconds in boiling water. Refresh under cold running water, drain and reserve.

Preheat the oven to 160°C (325°F). Lightly score the skin of each fillet of barramundi with a sharp knife and rub with a pinch of ground sea salt. Let the fish sit for a few minutes while you heat a small amount of olive oil in a frying pan. Fry the barramundi fillets over a medium heat, skin side down, until the skin begins to turn golden and crispy, about 5–8 minutes. Transfer the barramundi fillets to the oven and cook for 3–5 minutes, skin side down, until the flesh is cooked through. Remove from the oven and drain briefly on absorbent paper.

Meanwhile, heat the peanut oil in a wok, and stir-fry the Chinese broccoli stalks and leaves. Divide the steamed rice between 6 large bowls, accompanied by the Chinese broccoli. Arrange a barramundi fillet on top and pour over the yellow curry dressing. Garnish with a small amount of baby shoot salad and serve.

Serves 6

cheddar-grilled blue eye
with panzanella salad and olive oil

Panzanella

½ loaf day-old
casalinga bread

250 ml (9 fl oz)
clarified butter or ghee

100 ml (3½ fl oz)
olive oil

1 sprig fresh rosemary

2 cloves garlic

2 ripe tomatoes

1 long cucumber

2 red capsicums
(bell peppers)

1 teaspoon salted
capers, very well rinsed

1 teaspoon anchovies,
roughly chopped

½ bunch fresh
basil leaves

60 ml (2 fl oz)
extra-virgin olive oil

freshly ground
black pepper

**Cheddar-Grilled
Blue Eye**

50 ml (1½ fl oz)
olive oil

6 x 160 g (5½ oz)
blue eye fillets,
skin removed

salt and pepper

6 slices aged
cheddar cheese

Garnish

6 sprigs chervil

extra-virgin olive oil

Panzanella: Remove the crusts from the bread and cut it into 5 mm (¼ in) cubes. Leave the bread to dry out for an hour or so.

Put the clarified butter and olive oil in a large frying pan with the sprig of rosemary and the garlic cloves. Heat until it bubbles, and fry the cubes of bread in small batches until they turn golden brown and crunchy. Drain on absorbent paper and reserve. Reserve the rosemary for the salad.

Bring a large pot of water to the boil, blanch the tomatoes for 10 seconds then refresh in iced water. Peel them carefully, then cut in half, squeeze out the seeds and cut into 1 cm (½ in) dice. Peel the cucumber, slice out the seeds and cut into 1 cm (½ in) dice.

Preheat the oven to 200°C (400°F). Roast the capsicums for about 8 minutes, or until the skin blisters and blackens. When cool enough to handle, peel away the skin, remove the seeds and cut the capsicum into long strips.

Cheddar-Grilled Blue Eye: Preheat the oven to 200°C (400°F) and preheat the griller to its hottest temperature. Heat a little olive oil in a large frying pan. Season the blue eye fillets and arrange skin side down in the pan and cook until golden. Remove from heat put in oven and cook for 5–8 minutes, or until the fish is just cooked. Top each fish fillet with a slice of cheese and cook under the hot grill until the cheese starts to bubble and turn golden brown. Drain briefly on absorbent paper before serving.

In a large bowl, mix together all the panzanella salad ingredients. Toss with olive oil and season with pepper. Arrange a mound of salad in the centre of each plate and place a blue eye fillet on top. Garnish with chervil and a drizzle of extra-virgin olive oil.

Serves 6

crispy-skin ocean trout
with caper and soft herb mash, anchovy mayonnaise and citrus salsa

Caper and Soft Herb Mash

500 g (1 lb) mashed potato (see Basics)

2 tablespoons baby salted capers, very well rinsed

1 tablespoon finely chopped chives

1 tablespoon finely chopped dill

1 tablespoon finely chopped chervil

sea salt

freshly ground black pepper

Anchovy Mayonnaise

8 anchovies

1 egg yolk

1 teaspoon Dijon mustard

50 ml (1½ fl oz) white wine vinegar

250 ml (9 fl oz) olive oil

juice of ½ lemon

sea salt

freshly ground black pepper

Citrus Salsa

1 pink grapefruit

1 orange

1 lemon

1 lime

1 blood orange

2 golden shallots

2 teaspoons raspberry vinegar

50 ml (1½ fl oz) extra-virgin olive oil

Ocean Trout

6 x 160 g (5½ oz) ocean trout fillets, skin on and pin bones removed

50 ml (1½ fl oz) olive oil for frying

Caper and Soft Herb Mash: Follow the Basic recipe for mashed potatoes, and prepare the other ingredients.

Anchovy Mayonnaise: Pass the anchovies through a fine sieve to remove the bones. Place in a food processor with the egg yolk, Dijon mustard and white wine vinegar. Purée until smooth and creamy. Slowly add the oil until the mixture emulsifies and thickens. Add the lemon juice and season with salt and pepper to taste. The mayonnaise should be very thick, not runny. Spoon into a piping bag fitted with a very small plain nozzle.

Citrus Salsa: Peel the grapefruit, orange, lemon, lime and blood orange and carefully slice the segments of fruit out of their casings. Chop into even dice and place in a small dish. Add the finely diced shallots, the raspberry vinegar and olive oil and stir gently.

To Serve: Preheat the oven to 180°C (350°F). Heat the olive oil in a large ovenproof frying pan and cook the trout, skin side down, until it is crispy and golden brown, about 5 minutes. Transfer to the oven and bake for 6 minutes, until the trout is cooked medium.

Warm the mash and stir in the capers and finely chopped herbs. Taste and season with pepper and extra salt if necessary.

Pipe the anchovy mayonnaise onto each plate in a zig-zag pattern. Place a spoonful of mash in the centre of each plate and arrange the trout on top. Sprinkle the citrus salsa over the trout and serve immediately.

Serves 6

grilled swordfish

with baked eggplant, whipped mascarpone and goat's cheese, red piperade and balsamic syrup

Red Piperade

4 medium red
capsicums
(bell peppers)

100 ml (3½ fl oz)
balsamic vinegar

75g (3 oz) sugar

1 medium brown
onion, finely sliced

salt and pepper

Baked Eggplant

2 medium eggplants
(aubergines)

100 ml (3½ fl oz)
extra-virgin olive oil

Whipped Mascarpone and Goat's Cheese

1 cup goat's cheese,
at room temperature

½ cup mascarpone,
at room temperature

1 tablespoon
chopped chives

1 tablespoon
chopped dill

1 tablespoon
chopped chervil

juice of ½ lemon

sea salt

freshly ground
black pepper

Grilled Swordfish

6 x 160 g (5½ oz)
swordfish steaks
from loin

30 ml (1 fl oz)
extra-virgin olive oil

sea salt

Garnish

balsamic syrup
(see Basics)

100 ml (3½ fl oz)
extra-virgin olive oil

My head chef Brendan McQueen created this dish in his early days at ezard. I was particularly delighted to see him using my favourite sweet-sour flavour combination in a Mediterranean dish instead of the Asian style we normally adopt. I love this dish – the sweetness and acidity of the piperade and the tangy balsamic dressing are perfect counterpoints to the creamy blandness of the whipped cheeses and cut the oily meatiness of the swordfish.

Red Piperade: Preheat oven to 200°C (400°F). Place each capsicum in a brown paper bag, seal and roast in the oven for 10–15 minutes. Remove from the bags and when cool enough to handle, carefully peel away the skin from each capsicum. Cut in half, scrape away the seeds and slice into julienne strips. Place the balsamic vinegar and sugar in a non-reactive saucepan and bring to a gentle simmer. Add the capsicum and onion and cook slowly for 20–30 minutes. Remove from the heat and allow to cool. Taste and season if necessary.

Baked Eggplant: Preheat the oven to 200°C (400°F). Slice the eggplants into 2.5 cm (1 in) thick discs, one per person. Brush generously with olive oil and sprinkle with salt. Heat the remaining oil in an ovenproof frying pan and fry the eggplant slices on both sides until they are golden brown, about 3 minutes. Transfer the eggplant to the oven and cook for a further 3–4 minutes, until the flesh is tender, and the skin is a glossy dark brown all over. Drain on absorbent paper and keep warm.

Whipped Mascarpone and Goat's Cheese: Place the goat's cheese in a large mixing bowl and break down with a wooden spoon. Add the mascarpone and whisk the two cheeses together until smooth and creamy. Add the chopped herbs and lemon juice and mix together well. Season with salt and pepper to taste and refrigerate.

To Serve: Heat a griddle pan or barbecue and brush with olive oil. Brush a little oil on each swordfish steak and sprinkle with sea salt. Sear the swordfish steaks for 1–2 minutes on each side, until evenly coloured. This should be enough to cook them medium.

Place a slice of eggplant in the centre of each plate topped with a dollop of whipped mascarpone. Arrange the swordfish on top and spoon over the red piperade. Swirl some balsamic syrup and extra-virgin olive oil around the plates and serve.

Note: Marlin may be used instead of swordfish.

Serves 6

seared yellowfin tuna

with black bean dressing, potato and cucumber salad and crispy shiso leaf salad

Black Bean Dressing

1 red capsicum
(bell pepper)

1 tablespoon
olive oil

1 small red onion,
finely diced

2 cloves garlic, minced

30 g (1 oz) fresh ginger,
peeled and cut into
julienne strips

juice of 4 limes

70 ml (3 fl oz)
Japanese light
soy sauce

20 ml (¾ fl oz)
sweet soy sauce
(ketjap manis)

2 teaspoons salted
black beans

Potato and Cucumber Salad

300 g (10 oz)
southern gold
potatoes, unpeeled

18 asparagus spears

1 long cucumber

30 ml (1 fl oz)
olive oil

salt and pepper

Crispy Shiso Leaf Salad

1 litre (1¾ pints)
vegetable oil for frying

15 wonton skins, chilled

½ cup coriander
(cilantro) leaves

1 cup shiso leaves

Tuna

6 x 150 g (5 oz)
yellowfin tuna steaks

Black Bean Dressing: Preheat the oven to 200ºC (400ºF). Brush the capsicum with the olive oil and roast until the skin starts to blister and peel away, 10–15 minutes. When cool enough to handle, carefully pull away the skin and scrape out the seeds. Dice the capsicum and place in a large mixing bowl. Add the red onion, garlic and ginger, pour on the lime juice and both soy sauces and mix everything together well. Add the black beans, toss through lightly, taste and adjust seasoning if necessary. Reserve at room temperature.

Potato and Cucumber Salad : Bring a large pot of salted water to the boil and cook the potatoes until tender. Drain and peel the potatoes, then cut them into bite-size pieces.

Snap off the woody ends of the asparagus and peel them two-thirds of the way up the stalk. Bring a fresh pot of salted water to the boil and blanch the asparagus for 1–2 minutes, depending on the thickness of the stalks. Refresh in iced water, drain well and cut each stalk into bite-size pieces.

Peel and seed the cucumber and cut into bite-size pieces.

Crispy Shiso Leaf Salad: Heat the vegetable oil to 180ºC (350ºF) in a large frying pan or wok. Slice the wonton skins as thinly as possible, into hair-like strands. Sprinkle the shredded wontons into the hot oil and fry in small batches, for 20–30 seconds until crispy. Drain on absorbent paper.

To Serve: Bring a pot of water to the boil. Mix the potato, asparagus and cucumber together in a steamer basket and gently warm through. Lightly toss with olive oil and season with salt and pepper.

Meanwhile, heat a large frying pan or wok to the highest possible temperature – you will need it to be almost white-hot. Briefly sear the tuna, about 20 seconds on each side for medium.

Spoon a generous mound of potato salad onto the centre of each plate. Arrange a tuna steak on top and pour over the black bean dressing. Mix the coriander and shiso leaves with the crispy wontons and place a small handful on top of each tuna steak.

Note: Ask your fishmonger cut the tuna into 6 steaks. Ensure that this is carried out in front of you, so you know that the tuna is freshly cut.

Serves 6

hot – cold
combinations

Combining hot and cold components in a dish is another way of introducing some excitement to the palate. It is a classic technique in Asian cooking where balancing yin and yang is all-important.

It is very easy to achieve this kind of balance in a dish, and in reality it is something most of us do intuitively. Hot spicy foods, for instance, cry out for something cool and refreshing to balance them.

Combining hot and cold elements in a dish might be something as simple as serving a little salad with a piece of grilled fish. Other good examples from the recipes in this book include the Chilli Salt Squid with Asian Herb Salad (see page 61). This dish combines hot and spicy deep-fried rings of squid with a cool, refreshing salad dressed with a tangy-sweet dressing.

Other great examples of the way hot and cold elements of a dish complement each other beautifully are the Crispy Fried Pork Hock with Chilli Caramel, Steamed Rice and Spicy Thai Salad (see page 121) and the Coconut Fried Garfish with Vietnamese Rice Noodle Salad and Hot Tamarind Dressing (see page 91).

seaweed and dashi salt tuna
with sweet and sour cucumbers, wasabi mash and pickled ginger juice dressing

Sweet and Sour Cucumbers

2 long cucumbers

100 ml (3½ fl oz) peanut oil

200 ml (7 fl oz) water

200 ml (7 fl oz) rice wine vinegar

200 g (7 oz) sugar

6 cloves garlic, finely sliced

3 red bird's eye chillies, finely sliced

1 red Lombok chilli, finely sliced

1½ tablespoons grated ginger

½ teaspoon black sesame seeds

Dashi Salt

2 sheets of nori

1 tablespoon dashi

2 tablespoons bonito

2 tablespoons sea salt

Pickled Ginger Juice

200 ml (7 fl oz) juice from pickled ginger (see Basics)

Wasabi Mash

400 g (14 oz) mashed potatoes (see Basics)

2 teaspoons wasabi paste

sea salt

Tuna

6 x 150 g (5 oz) tuna steaks

This dish is a real favourite of mine because of the elegant simplicity of its flavours. The refreshing pickled elements cut through the oiliness of the tuna fish, while the wasabi mash adds a real fiery kick.

Sweet and Sour Cucumbers: Peel the cucumbers and slice them into long fine shreds, using a mandolin if possible. Bring a medium pot of water to the boil and blanch the cucumber for 5–10 seconds then refresh in iced water. Drain well and transfer to a large mixing bowl.

Put the peanut oil, water, rice wine vinegar and sugar into a large non-reactive saucepan. Add 2 of the sliced garlic cloves and 1 of the red bird's eye chillies. Bring to the boil, cook for 3–4 minutes then remove from the heat and allow the preserving liquid to cool completely. When cold, strain onto the cucumbers.

Add the remaining garlic and chillies to the preserved cucumbers with the ginger and black sesame seeds and stir together well. Refrigerate until ready to serve.

Dashi Salt: Using a pair of scissors, cut the nori sheets into very small pieces. Place in a spice grinder or vitamiser with the dashi and bonito flakes and blitz to a powder. Tip into a large mixing bowl, stir in the sea salt and reserve.

To Serve: Heat the mashed potatoes and mix in the wasabi paste until well combined. Season to taste.

Meanwhile, heat a large frying pan or wok to the highest possible temperature – you will need it to be almost white-hot. Briefly sear the tuna, about 20 seconds on each side for medium.

Spoon a generous amount of wasabi mash into each shallow bowl, and stand the tuna steak upright next to it. Top each tuna steak with a tablespoon of sweet and sour cucumbers. Sprinkle with dashi salt, drizzle over a small amount of ginger juice and serve straight away.

Note: Ask your fishmonger to cut the tuna into 6 steaks. Ensure that this is carried out in front of you, so you know that the tuna is freshly cut.

Serves 6

crispy-skin salmon
with skordalia, aioli and crispy onion and herb salad

Salmon

1 whole fillet Tasmanian salmon, 1.2 kg (2½ lb), skin on

50 ml (1½ fl oz) olive oil

sea salt

Aioli

½ head of garlic

1 egg yolk

1 tablespoon white wine vinegar

1 tablespoon Dijon mustard

225 ml (7½ fl oz) olive oil

1 tablespoon hot water

sea salt

Crispy Onion and Herb Salad

1 litre (1¾ pints) vegetable oil

2 large brown onions, very finely sliced

½ teaspoon freshly ground sea salt

½ teaspoon caster (superfine) sugar

½ cup chives

½ cup dill

½ cup chervil

40 ml (1½ fl oz) extra-virgin olive oil

2 lemons, peeled, segmented and diced

Skordalia

600 g (1¼ lb) peeled potatoes

100 ml (3½ fl oz) milk

4 cloves garlic, bruised

juice of 1 lemon

30 ml (1 fl oz) extra-virgin olive oil

sea salt

freshly ground black pepper

Salmon: Remove the pin bones from the salmon fillet and scrape away any fish scales. Rinse and dry thoroughly then cut into 6 x 160–180 g (5½–6 oz) portions.

Aioli: Preheat the oven to 150ºC (300ºF). Wrap the garlic in a piece of lightly greased kitchen foil and roast until tender, about 30 minutes. Remove from the oven and allow to cool in the foil, then scrape the soft garlic away from the skins into a food processor. Add the egg yolk, white wine vinegar and mustard and purée until the mixture thickens and nearly doubles in size. Slowly add the oil until the mixture emulsifies and thickens, and stir in a tablespoon of hot water. Season to taste. Scrape the aioli into a piping bag with a very small round nozzle and refrigerate until needed.

Crispy Onion and Herb Salad: Heat the vegetable oil in a saucepan or deep fryer to 160ºC (325ºF). Fry the onions in several small batches until deep brown. Remove with a slotted spoon and drain on absorbent paper. Spread them out evenly and season with salt and sugar and store in a dry place until needed.

Skordalia: Bring a large pan of salted water to the boil and cook the potatoes until tender. Tip the potatoes into a colander to drain and allow them to sit for a few minutes to steam dry.

Put the milk and bruised garlic cloves in a small saucepan. Bring to a gentle simmer and infuse milk for 5–6 minutes. Remove from the heat and infuse for a further 3–4 minutes.

Pass the potatoes through a sieve or potato ricer into a large mixing bowl. Strain the hot milk onto the potatoes, a little at a time, and whisk in to form a smooth purée. Add lemon juice, olive oil, salt and pepper to taste. Keep warm until ready to serve.

To Serve: Preheat the oven to 200ºC (400ºF). To cook the salmon, heat the olive oil in a large ovenproof frying pan. Season the salmon fillets with freshly ground sea salt and place in the pan, skin side down. Cook 3–4 minutes on a low heat until the skin turns crispy and brown. Transfer to the oven and cook for a further 3 minutes. Remove from the oven and allow to rest for 1–2 minutes on absorbent paper before serving. The salmon should be cooked medium-rare so that it is still quite pink in the centre.

Use the piping bag to zig-zag the aioli across each plate. Place a neat scoop of skordalia in the centre and arrange a piece of salmon on top. Mix together the crispy onions and fresh herbs and place a small handful on top of each piece of salmon. Drizzle some extra-virgin olive oil around the plate, some diced lemon and serve immediately.

Serves 6

red roast baby chicken
with prickly ash, green nam jim, sweet soy and chilli sambal

Red Roast Chicken	Green Nam Jim	Chilli Sambal	Sweet Soy Garnish
6 x 500 g (1 lb) whole baby chickens	3 long green chillies, seeded and roughly chopped	½ teaspoon shrimp paste	100 ml (3½ fl oz) light soy sauce
150 g (5 oz) fresh ginger, roughly sliced	3 green bird's eye chillies, roughly chopped	1 teaspoon peanut oil	100 ml (3½ fl oz) Japanese soy sauce (tamari)
½ bunch spring onions (scallions), roughly chopped	2 teaspoons roughly chopped fresh ginger	3 red shallots, finely sliced	100 ml (3½ fl oz) sweet soy sauce (ketjap manis)
3 litres (6 pints) master stock (see Basics)	1 small red shallot, roughly chopped	2 teaspoons finely chopped ginger	200 g (7 oz) jasmine rice (see Basics)
3 limes	1 clove garlic, roughly chopped	3 red bird's eye chillies, finely chopped	200 ml (7 fl oz) water
3 litres (6 pints) vegetable oil for deep-frying	3 coriander (cilantro) roots, roughly chopped	3 fresh kaffir lime leaves, finely chopped	
2 tablespoons prickly ash (see Basics)	50 g (2 oz) peanut praline (see Basics)	1 stalk lemongrass, white part only, finely chopped	
	125 ml (4 fl oz) lime juice, about 8 limes	1 tablespoon lime juice	
	2 tablespoons fish sauce	1 teaspoon fish sauce	
		gula melaka syrup to taste (see Basics)	

I love this dish as it incorporates several different Asian techniques and flavour combinations. The chicken is prepared in a Chinese manner, the nam jim is a favourite Thai sauce and the sambal accompaniment is an authentic recipe I learnt during a trip to the Casa Luna cooking school in Bali.

This dish is all about the way the various exciting flavours come together. It is best eaten in the traditional Asian way – with your hands – so you can combine the flavours to your own particular taste.

Red Roast Chicken: Use a sharp knife to trim the wing tips from the baby chickens. Rinse and thoroughly dry the birds, inside and out, then stuff the ginger and spring onions into the cavities. Use toothpicks to tightly seal each opening.

In a large saucepan bring the master stock to the boil. Add the baby chickens, making sure they are completely covered by stock. Poach the chickens for 30 minutes, then turn off the heat and allow them to cool in the stock. When completely cold, carefully lift out each bird, being careful not to tear the skin. Keep them chilled until ready to fry. The master stock can be re-used in another chicken dish. Bring the stock back to the boil, skim it well then strain into a container and refrigerate or freeze.

Green Nam Jim: Use a mortar and pestle to pound the chillies, ginger, shallot, garlic and coriander roots to a smooth paste. Add the peanut praline and pound it into the paste. Then slowly add the lime juice and fish sauce, a little at a time, until you achieve a good balance of sweet, hot and spicy. This green nam jim is very refreshing.

Chilli Sambal: Preheat the oven to 180ºC (350ºF). Wrap the shrimp paste in a piece of kitchen foil and roast until fragrant, about 4–6 minutes.

Heat the oil in a medium-size saucepan and gently sweat the shallots, ginger, chillies, lime leaves and lemongrass until fragrant, about 5 minutes. Stir constantly to ensure the ingredients don't catch on the bottom of the pan and burn. Add the shrimp paste and cook a further 3–4 minutes. Tip the mixture into a mortar and pound to a very smooth paste. Season with lime juice and fish sauce to taste. Just before serving, add the gula melaka to taste to balance the flavours.

Sweet Soy Garnish: Whisk together the three soy sauces and keep until ready to serve.

To Serve: Wash the jasmine rice in a colander until the water runs clear. Place in a rice cooker, add the cold water and steam until tender (see Basics).

Preheat the oven to 120ºC (245ºF). Heat the vegetable oil to 180ºC (350ºF) in a large saucepan or deep-fryer. Fry the baby chickens, no more than 2–3 at a time, until they turn crispy and golden brown, around 7–8 minutes. Remove from the oil and rest on absorbent paper. Keep warm in the oven while you cook the remaining chickens.

Carefully remove the toothpicks from each chicken and use a sharp heavy knife to cut down each side of the backbone. Neatly remove it, together with the rib cage, and discard the ginger and spring onion. Season the chickens liberally with prickly ash.

Lay a circle of banana leaf on each plate and place the chicken on top. Serve with the steamed jasmine rice with chilli sambal on top, and little individual bowls of green nam jim, sweet soy sauce and prickly ash.

Note: It is much better if you have a deep fryer, as you can cook several chickens at once.

Serves 6

spiced salts

Spiced salts are a really interesting way of seasoning food and they are something I use a great deal in my cooking. Salt is the universal seasoning used all around the world to heighten the flavour of foods. (It also has very useful preserving qualities.) I always use the best quality salt flakes I can find as it has an incomparable flavour.

Spiced salts are used frequently in Asian cuisines. For instance, Chinese roasted and barbecued meats are nearly always accompanied by a little dish of salt flavoured with Sichuan peppercorns and five-spice powder. Japanese cooking is rather more purist, relying mainly on the natural flavours of each ingredient, but one well-loved seasoning is sesame salt, goma shio, which adds a delicious nutty dimension to a dish.

One of my favourite spiced salts is prickly ash; so called because the Sichuan pepper really does prickle the tongue. It's another essential seasoning in my restaurant and is really, really good with crispy-skin dishes – especially fried quail and duck.

I also like to bring out the flavours of the sea in seafood dishes by serving them with a bonito-dashi spiced salt! Roasted rice is another favourite of mine. It is very versatile and I use it to make a crispy coating for fish (see Baby Snapper with Roasted Rice Crust, page 84) but also as a garnish to sprinkle over salads and other dishes. It has a wonderful toasted nutty flavour and adds a really unusual grainy texture and crunch to a dish.

I really love the idea of using spiced salts – in fact the first thing you find on the table when you dine at ezard restaurant, is a little trio of condiment dishes. One contains a mixture of yellow sugar and dried chillies, and the other two contain spiced salts. One is flavoured with seaweed and dashi, the other with Sichuan pepper. I strongly encourage diners to experiment with these seasonings throughout the meal.

soy-glazed chicken breast
with warm rice noodle salad and spicy fried peanut, lime and coriander dressing

Spicy Fried Peanut, Lime and Coriander Dressing

250 ml (7 fl oz) peanut oil

3 cloves garlic, finely chopped

20 g (¾ oz) fresh ginger, peeled and finely chopped

2 red bird's eye chillies, finely chopped

75 g (3½ oz) roasted unsalted peanuts, roughly chopped

125 ml (4 fl oz) mirin

salt

1 bunch spring onions (scallions), white ends only, finely chopped

1 bunch coriander (cilantro), roots and stalks only, finely chopped

zest of 2 limes (reserve juice for garnish)

3 fresh kaffir lime leaves, finely shredded

1 lemongrass stalk, white part only, finely chopped

30 ml (1 fl oz) light soy sauce

2 teaspoons grated palm sugar

Warm Rice Noodle Salad

50 g (2 oz) dried rice-stick noodles

1 teaspoon peanut oil

50 g (1¾ oz) snow peas

1 bunch kai-lum, (or Chinese broccoli) leaves only, finely shredded

½ bunch spring onions (scallions), white ends only, finely sliced

salt and pepper

Soy Glaze

50 g (2 oz) honey

75 ml (3 fl oz sweet soy sauce (ketjap manis)

100 ml (3½ fl oz) light soy sauce

Garnish

30 ml (1 fl oz) lime juice

20 ml (¾ fl oz) fish sauce

3 tablespoons Vietnamese mint leaves

3 tablespoons coriander (cilantro) leaves

Chicken

6 x 160 g (5½ oz) chicken breasts, skin on

50 ml (1½ fl oz) olive oil

Spicy Fried Peanut, Lime and Coriander Dressing: Heat the peanut oil in a wok or large saucepan. Fry the garlic, ginger and chillies until fragrant, about 2–3 minutes. Add the chopped peanuts and fry until they turn a nice golden brown. Add the mirin, warm gently, and light with a match to burn off the alcohol. When the flames disappear strain the liquid through a sieve into a clean saucepan. Drain the fried peanut mixture on absorbent paper and season with salt. Keep these spicy peanuts to add to the dressing before serving.

Add the spring onions, coriander root, lime zest, kaffir lime leaves, lemongrass, soy sauce and palm sugar to the reserved liquid and allow to sit for a couple of hours to let the flavours develop and intensify.

Warm Rice Noodle Salad: Bring a small pot of water to the boil. Add the rice-stick noodles, then remove the pot from the heat and allow the noodles to soak in the hot water for 3–4 minutes, or until they are tender. Refresh under cold water, then drain thoroughly. Tip the noodles into a mixing bowl and stir through the peanut oil.

Blanch the snow peas for 5 seconds then refresh under cold running water. Shred them lengthways and add to the rice-stick noodles with the kai-lum and spring onions. Toss together well and keep at room temperature until ready to serve.

Soy Glaze: Heat the honey and soy sauces in a shallow saucepan. Simmer until it just starts to smoke. Watch very carefully and remove from the heat as soon as the glaze darkens and begins to caramelise (be careful not to let it burn). As it cools, the glaze will become sticky and jam-like. Tip into a small container and reserve.

To Serve: Preheat the oven to 180°C (350°F). Heat the oil in a large frying pan and fry the chicken breasts, skin side down, until they turn golden brown. Transfer the chicken breasts to the oven for about 10 minutes, or until just cooked. Keep warm and allow to rest for a further 10 minutes. Meanwhile, preheat the grill to its hottest temperature. Just before you are ready to serve, drizzle the chicken breasts liberally with soy glaze and place under the grill for a minute to caramelise.

Pour the dressing into a non-reactive saucepan and warm very gently so as to preserve the intensity of the flavours. When just luke-warm, add the fried peanut mix to the dressing and season with the lime juice and fish sauce. Finally add the mint and coriander leaves.

Arrange the warm rice noodle salad on each plate. Place a piece of soy-glazed chicken on top, spoon over the spicy peanut dressing and serve immediately.

Note: Once the base for the dressing is cooked, it is best to allow it to sit for a few hours so the flavours can develop and intensify. When re-heating, make sure not to let the dressing boil – it should really just be luke-warm. The lime juice and fish sauce should be added at the very last moment, just before serving.

Serves 6

crispy duck and wonton stack
with water spinach, candied chillies, sticky soy and sesame oil dressing

Crispy Duck

200 ml (7 fl oz) maltose

50 ml (1¾ fl oz) rice wine vinegar

200 ml (7 fl oz) water

1 x 1.6 kg (3 lb) whole pekin duck, neck attached

30 g (1 oz) fresh ginger, roughly chopped

½ bunch spring onions, roughly chopped

2 star anise

½ cup Shao Xing wine

Sesame Dressing

100 ml (3½ fl oz) peanut oil

25 ml (1 fl oz) sesame oil

2 cloves garlic, finely chopped

30 g (1 oz) fresh ginger, finely chopped

1 red Lombok chilli, finely sliced

juice of ½ lemon

50 ml (1¾ fl oz) light soy sauce

2 teaspoons white sesame seeds

Spicy Wontons

18 wonton skins

1 litre (2 pints) vegetable oil for frying

1 teaspoon dried chilli

1 tablespoon Sichuan peppercorns

1 whole nutmeg

3 cinnamon sticks

5 star anise

1 tablespoon cardamom pods

3 tablespoons salt flakes

Water Spinach Salad

100 g (3½ oz) vermicelli rice noodles

1 large red onion

1 long cucumber

50 g (1¾ oz) water chestnuts

2 teaspoons white sesame seeds

1 cup watercress leaves

1 cup coriander leaves

1 bunch water spinach, leaves only

50 g (1¾ oz) candied chillies (see Basics)

Garnish

150 ml (5 fl oz) sticky soy (see Basics)

This is a fabulous dish; it is visually very appealing with great flavour combinations. The crispy duck is prepared in the traditional pekin style. It is for the determined and serious cook as it is quite time-consuming and a little tricky to prepare. For the less adventurous, Chinese-style roast duck is readily available from Chinatown, and will substitute quite satisfactorily.

Crispy Duck: Place the maltose, vinegar and water in a non-reactive saucepan and bring to the boil. Remove from the heat and reserve.

Trim the wing tips from the duck. Rinse and thoroughly dry the duck, inside and out, and place on its back on a clean work surface.

In a small bowl, mix together the chopped ginger, spring onions and star anise, and spoon the mixture into the cavity of the duck. Carefully pour the Shao Xing wine into the cavity too, and use metal skewers through the flaps of skin to seal the opening completely.

Loosely tie a piece of butcher's twine around the neck of the duck. Make a small incision in the skin, behind the piece of twine, carefully insert the nozzle of a bicycle pump and pump to inflate the skin. This is what helps the duck to crisp up as it cooks. Withdraw the pump and tie the twine tightly, trapping the air under the skin.

Carefully transfer the duck, still on its back, to a baking tray. Bring the maltose syrup back to the boil and pour a little over the duck. Return it to the heat and when it boils again, pour a little more over the duck. Repeat this procedure several times more, until the flesh of the duck tightens. Place the duck in front of a fan for 2 hours to dry.

Preheat the oven to 200ºC (400ºF). Place a small baking tray filled with water on the bottom of the oven. Roast the duck for 15 minutes, then lower the temperature to 170ºC (325ºF) and roast for a further 40 minutes. The initial blast of heat will cook the skin quickly and steam the flesh inside. Remove the duck from the oven, cut away the twine and remove the skewers. Let the duck rest for at least 20 minutes before carving. Once the duck is cool, carefully bone out the duck legs and breasts.

Sesame Dressing: Place the peanut oil, sesame oil, garlic, ginger and chilli into a saucepan and heat on a high flame to infuse the oil with the aromatic ingredients. Stir from time to time so they don't burn. As soon as the aromatics start to colour remove the pan from the heat. Allow to cool a little, then strain the infused oil into a clean jar. Add the lemon juice to taste together with the light soy sauce. Lightly toast the sesame seeds and add them to the dressing.

Spicy Wontons: Heat the oil to 160°C (325°F) degrees. Fry the wonton skins, a few at a time, for about 30 seconds on each side. Make sure they stay flat in the cooking oil – if the oil is too hot, they are likely to bend and become misshapen. Remove from the oil and drain on absorbent paper.

Toast the spices in a hot oven until they are fragrant, then grind them finely in a mortar and pestle or a spice grinder. Season with the spicy salt.

Water Spinach Salad: Blanch the rice vermicelli in boiling water for a few seconds until al dente, then gently rinse under cold running water. Slice the red onion as finely as possible using a Japanese binriner or a very sharp knife. Peel the cucumber and slice into long, thin hair-like strands. Drain the water chestnuts and cut them into ½ cm (¼ in) dice. Lightly toast the sesame seeds. Place all the salad ingredients in a mixing bowl and toss gently, so they are well combined.

To Serve: Preheat the griller to its hottest temperature. Arrange the duck pieces on a flat baking tray lined with foil and place under the grill to warm through and crisp up the skin. Transfer to absorbent paper to drain off any excess fat. Allow to cool slightly, then break legs into small bite-sized pieces and slice the breast lengthways.

Lay the wontons on a flat surface and sprinkle them with the ground spice mix.

Toss the salad with the sesame dressing, adjusting the balance of flavours to your taste. Divide the salad into 6 even portions. Toss each portion with an equal amount of duck.

To serve, swirl a spiral of sticky soy around each plate and place a spicy wonton skin in the centre. Carefully pile a little mound of duck salad on top of each spicy wonton, then top with another spicy wonton and another portion of salad. Finish each stack with a final spicy wonton.

Serves 6

duck san choi bao
with oyster sauce and chinese flavours

Duck

6 duck legs

1½ litres (2½ pints) Asian-style duck stock (see Basics)

Pork

1 teaspoon olive oil

3 red shallots, finely chopped

3 spring onions (scallions), white part only, finely chopped

3 cloves garlic, finely chopped

40 g (1½ oz) fresh ginger, peeled and finely chopped

350 g (12 oz) pork mince

30 ml (1 fl oz) Chinese cooking wine

Salad

8 dried shiitake mushrooms

8 fresh shiitake mushrooms, finely chopped

3 dried Chinese pork sausages, finely sliced

8 water chestnuts, finely chopped

5 medium spring onions (scallions), finely sliced

4 coriander (cilantro) roots, finely sliced

Oyster Sauce

300 ml (10½ fl oz) duck braising liquid

100 ml (3½ fl oz) Chinese cooking wine

100 ml (3½ fl oz) oyster sauce

Garnish

2 small iceberg lettuces, outer leaves removed

2 teaspoons sesame seeds

Duck: Preheat the oven to 160°C (325°F). Sear the duck legs in a hot dry frying pan until they turn golden brown and the fat starts to render, about 5 minutes. Transfer to a large deep braising dish. Bring the duck stock to the boil and strain over the duck legs. Cover the braising dish tightly with a lid or kitchen foil and cook until the duck legs are tender and the meat is starting to fall from the bone, about 1½ hours.

Remove from the oven and allow the duck legs to cool in the braising liquid. When they are completely cold, carefully scrape off any surface fat that may have formed and remove the ducks from the liquid. Chop the duck meat into bite-size pieces and refrigerate. Strain the duck braising liquid and keep for adding to the oyster sauce.

Pork: Heat the olive oil in a large frying pan and fry the shallots, spring onions, garlic and ginger until fragrant, 2–3 minutes. Add the pork mince and fry for 5 minutes. Deglaze the pan with Chinese cooking wine, and steam the mixture for 5 minutes. The wine adds flavour and also helps break down the pork mince as it cooks. You may need to add more – it evaporates quickly. Remove from the heat, allow to cool then refrigerate until ready to serve.

Salad: Place the dried shiitake mushrooms in a small bowl and pour on enough warm water just to cover them. Soak for 15–20 minutes, or until very soft. Squeeze out excess water and finely chop the mushrooms. Mix with the fresh shiitake mushrooms. Prepare other salad ingredients and keep until ready to serve.

Oyster Sauce: Heat 300 ml (10½ fl oz) of the reserved duck braising liquid in a small pan, skimming off any excess fat. Reduce by two-thirds, and stir in the Chinese cooking wine and oyster sauce and keep warm.

Garnish: Cut the iceberg lettuces in half and break the leaves away carefully, keeping them intact. You will need 18 leaves in total, 3 per person.

Preheat the oven to 200°C (400°F) and lightly toast the sesame seeds until fragrant and golden brown.

To Serve: In a large bowl mix together the duck meat, cooked pork and the salad ingredients. Heat the oil in a wok and fry the mixture in small batches until the meat is coloured. Add a little oyster sauce to moisten, and keep warm while frying the remaining mixture. Serve in bowls, topped with a sprinkling of sesame seeds and accompanied by the lettuce cups.

Serves 6

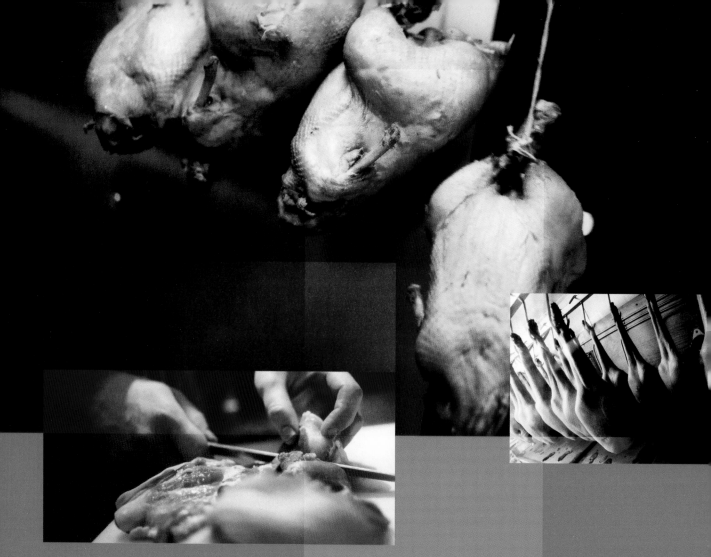

red braising
and red roasting

I first learnt about red-braising during a visit to Hong Kong and China. I was lucky enough to be able to visit a number of restaurant kitchens there and was always bowled over by the amazing aromas that filled the air. I quickly found out that the source of these incredible smells was an Asian master stock – an essential stock in all Chinese kitchens. These stocks are treated very reverentially and can live forever. In Chinese homes, a master stock may even be passed down several generations.

An Asian master stock is an extraordinarily flavoursome base stock used for Chinese red-cooked dishes. It is flavoured with soy sauce, Chinese wine, rock sugar and many different aromatics. The soy sauce imparts a distinctive shiny, reddish-brown colour to food while the other ingredients all contribute to the intense flavour. See page 3 for a detailed recipe.

In red-braised dishes, larger cuts of meat and poultry are cooked long and slowly in a master stock. The stock penetrates the flesh and results in very tender, almost velvety meat.

Another cooking technique, known as red-roasting, is popular in Chinese restaurant kitchens. This involves roasting food that has been red-braised in a master stock. It delivers fantastically succulent meat or poultry, with shiny skin that almost looks lacquered. The average Chinese home doesn't have an oven, so a similar result is achieved by deep-frying red-braised cuts in oil in a wok.

crispy fried pork hock
with chilli caramel, steamed rice and spicy thai salad

Pork Hock

(Needs 12 hours)

3 x 500 g (1 lb)
boneless pork hocks

3 litres (6 pints) master
stock (see Basics)

3 litres (6 pints)
vegetable oil for frying

Chilli Caramel Sauce

500 g (1 lb) light palm
sugar, roughly chopped

450 ml (14½ fl oz) water

2 red bird's eye chillies,
finely sliced

2 long red chillies,
finely sliced

1 long green chilli,
finely sliced

40 ml (1¼ fl oz)
fish sauce

60 ml (2 fl oz)
lime juice

Spicy Thai Salad

3 fresh kaffir lime leaves

1 long cucumber,
peeled and finely sliced
on an angle

40 g (1½ oz) fresh ginger,
peeled and finely sliced

1 long red chilli, seeded
and finely sliced

1 lemongrass stalk, white
part only, finely chopped

1 small red onion, cut
in half and finely sliced

5 medium spring onions
(scallions), white ends only,
finely sliced on an angle

½ cup coriander
(cilantro) leaves

½ cup Thai basil leaves

½ cup mint leaves

1 cup pickled bean
shoots (see Basics)

¼ cup crispy shallot
garnish (see Basics)

Dressing

4 teaspoons lime juice

2 teaspoons fish sauce

2 teaspoons gula
melaka syrup
(see Basics)

Garnish

200 g (7 oz) jasmine rice

200 ml (7 fl oz) water

This is another of my signature dishes – the chilli-caramel flavours are really delicious with the crispy pork. At ezard restaurant we try to be as authentic as possible when using Asian master stocks. These add a truly extraordinary depth of flavour and colour to a dish, which only intensifies with time. Our master stock is in its third year!

Pork Hock: Preheat the oven to 150ºC (300ºF). Bring the master stock to the boil. Lay out three pieces of muslin on your work surface. Place a pork hock, skin side down, on each piece of muslin and roll up to form a neat sausage. Tuck in the ends of the muslin and tie securely with butcher's string. Place the hocks into a large deep braising dish and pour over the boiling stock. Cover with a lid, place in the oven and braise very slowly for 2–3 hours, or until the meat is tender. Remove from the oven and allow the pork hocks to cool in the braising liquid. When the hocks are cold, remove them from the liquid and let them drain in a colander. Pat them dry and refrigerate for at least 12 hours (or hang them in a cool dry place). Peel away the muslin and slice each hock into 4 even pieces, each around 200 g (7 oz).

Chilli Caramel Sauce: Place the palm sugar in a wide heavy-based saucepan. Add 400 ml (13 fl oz) water, bring to the boil and simmer for around 10 minutes to form a light caramel. Brush down the sides of the pan with water from time to time to stop it from crystallising. As the caramel starts to darken, remove the pan from the heat and add the remaining 50 ml (1½ fl oz) cold water, which will slow the cooking process. The caramel should be dark, but not burnt. Add the chillies and allow the caramel to cool. Season with the fish sauce and lime juice, tasting to check the balance of flavours, which should be hot, sweet and salty.

Spicy Thai Salad: Blanch the lime leaves in boiling water for 5 seconds, refresh in cold water and slice finely. Assemble and prepare the remaining salad ingredients. Prepare the pickled bean shoots and crispy shallots according to Basic recipes.

Garnish: Wash the jasmine rice in a colander until the water runs clear. Place in a rice cooker, add the cold water and steam until tender.

To Serve: In a medium saucepan or deep-fryer heat the vegetable oil to 180ºC (350ºF). Fry the pork, 2–3 pieces at a time, for 7–8 minutes, or until the skin turns a glossy dark brown. Remove from the oil and drain on absorbent paper. Keep warm while you fry the remaining pieces of pork.

Combine the salad ingredients in a large mixing bowl. To make the dressing, whisk together the lime juice, fish sauce and gula melaka. Taste and adjust the balance if necessary, pour onto the salad and mix everything together well.

Place a small mound of salad in the bottom of each bowl and top with a piece of pork. Drizzle with the chilli caramel and serve with steamed jasmine rice.

Note: The pork hocks may not initially appear to be crispy when they are removed from the oil. They will start to crisp up as they cool down out of the oil.

Serves 6

slow-cooking meat

Slow-cooking is a method I use a great deal in the restaurant. It is the perfect way to cook cuts of meat such as oxtail, beef shin, shanks, tongue or corned beef. The long slow cooking process is essential for breaking down the sinews in these tough cuts, and creates a meltingly soft and flavoursome result.

Slow-cooking is also an essential part of my favourite Chinese red-braising method. In this technique, larger cuts of meat and poultry are braised in an Asian master stock. The master stock is flavoured with soy sauce that gives the food a rich reddish-brown colour and with Chinese wine and rock sugar, which impart a unique flavour.

Aromatics are often added to the braising stock in slow-cooked dishes and they impregnate the food with flavour during the long cooking process. In Asian-style dishes I like to add aromatics such as garlic, ginger and chilli, while star anise, cinnamon, tamarind and dried mandarin peel add a spicy note. The braising stock for European dishes tend to be flavoured with a traditional mirepoix – the classic combination of chopped carrots, celery and onion – a bouquet garni and sometimes a splash of vinegar.

corned beef

with mustard mash, brown mushrooms, beans and crispy parsnips

Corned Beef

1.2–1.5 kg (2½–3 lb) pickled beef girello

2 medium carrots, roughly sliced

1 large brown onion, roughly sliced

½ head of celery, roughly chopped

50 ml (1¾ fl oz) white vinegar

Brown Mushroom Sauce

400 ml (14 fl oz) veal stock (see Basics)

100 ml (3½ fl oz) thickened cream

1 cup green beans

½ cup green lentils

100 g (3½ oz) Swiss brown mushrooms

1 tablespoon butter

Mustard Mash

500 g (1 lb) mashed potato (see Basics)

1 teaspoon Dijon mustard

2 teaspoons grain mustard

salt and pepper

Garnish

1 parsnip, trimmed and peeled

1 litre (2 pints) vegetable oil for frying

6 sprigs chervil

Corned Beef: Wrap the pickled beef girello in a clean tea towel and tie tightly with butcher's twine so that it will hold its shape during cooking. Place the pickled beef into a large non-reactive pot with the vegetables and cover with cold water and white vinegar. Bring to the boil then lower the heat to a simmer. Cook gently for 2–3 hours, or until the beef is tender. From time to time you will need to skim off any scum that floats to the surface. Remove the pan from the heat and allow the beef to cool completely in the stock. When cold, remove the beef from the stock, unwrap it from the tea towel and slice into 6 x 180 g (6 oz) portions. Place the beef portions back into the stock and reserve.

Brown Mushroom Sauce: Place the veal stock in a small saucepan and heat gently, skimming off any scum that rises to the surface. Reduce by half, then add the cream and reduce by half again. Strain the sauce through a fine sieve into a clean saucepan and season to taste. Reserve.

Blanch the beans in boiling water for 30 seconds then plunge them into iced water to refresh. Drain well and reserve.

Place the lentils in a small saucepan and cover with cold water. Simmer gently for about 20 minutes, or until tender. Tip the lentils into a sieve and rinse well under cold running water, which will stop the cooking process. Drain well and refrigerate.

Slice the mushrooms into quarters, discarding the stalks. Heat the batter and fry the mushrooms for 2–3 minutes in a hot dry frying pan, moving constantly, until they are evenly coloured and tender. Reserve.

Mustard Mash: Add both mustards to the mashed potatoes, mix well, season to taste and keep warm until ready to serve.

Garnish: Heat the oil in a medium-sized saucepan to 180°C (350°F). Slice the parsnip into long thin strips using a vegetable peeler or very sharp knife. Fry the parsnip 'crisps' so they colour evenly and retain their long shape. Remove from the oil and drain on kitchen paper. Store in a dry place.

To Serve: Gently reheat the corned beef portions in their cooking liquid, ensuring you don't let them boil. Gently reheat the sauce and add the beans, lentils and mushrooms. Heat the mustard mash, stirring constantly to make sure the mixture doesn't burn and stick to the bottom of the pan.

Spoon an even amount of mustard mash onto the centre of each bowl. Top with a portion of corned beef and pour a generous amount of the sauce over the beef and around the plate. Garnish with a little stack of parsnip 'crisps' and a sprig of chervil.

Serves 6

barbecued ox tongue
with southern gold potatoes, snake beans and sticky mustard dressing

Ox Tongue

(Needs 8 hours)

1 large pickled ox tongue (available from good butchers)

¼ head celery, trimmed and cut into 3 cm (1½ in) chunks

2 carrots, cut into 3 cm (1½ in) chunks

1 medium onion, cut into 3 cm (1½ in) chunks

1 leek, cut into 3 cm (1½ in) chunks

50 ml (1½ fl oz) white wine vinegar

salt

30 ml olive oil

Sticky Mustard Seed Dressing

250 ml (9 fl oz) white wine vinegar

150 ml (5 fl oz) champagne vinegar

100 ml (3½ fl oz) water

400 g (14 oz) caster (superfine) sugar

2 teaspoons dried yellow mustard seeds, soaked overnight in plenty of water

2 teaspoons grain mustard

Potato and Bean Salad

350 g (12 oz) southern gold potatoes

200 g (7 oz) snake beans, cut into 6 cm (2½ in) pieces

125 ml (4½ fl oz) clarified butter or ghee

20 ml (¾ fl oz) extra-virgin olive oil

Ox Tongue: Place the tongue in a large non-reactive saucepan with the celery, carrots, onion and leek and pour over enough cold water to cover. Add the vinegar and salt, cover the pot and bring to the boil. Turn down the heat and simmer gently for 2½–3 hours, or until the tongue is tender. Make sure the tongue remains covered with liquid – you may need to top it up from time to time. Test that the tongue is cooked by squeezing the centre part between your fingers – it should give easily under the pressure. Allow to cool in the cooking liquid and, while still warm, peel away the surface skin and any excess fat from the tongue. Refrigerate in the cooking liquid for at least 8 hours.

Remove cold tongue from cooking liquid and pat dry. Trim off the tip of the tongue and any excess fat or muscle tissue. Use your sharpest knife to cut the tongue crosswise into 5 mm (¼ in) slices. Refrigerate until ready to serve.

Sticky Mustard Seed Dressing: In a small non-reactive saucepan combine both vinegars, the water and sugar and simmer gently for about 10 minutes, or until reduced by around two-thirds. You may need to brush down the inside of the saucepan with cold water from time to time, to ensure the reduction does not crystallise. When cooked, the reduction should be a dense sticky syrup. Allow it to cool, then stir in the soaked and drained mustard seeds and the grain mustard and pour into a clean container. Store at room temperature until needed.

Potato and Bean Salad: Peel the potatoes and cook until tender, then drain and allow to cool. Cut the potatoes into slices, around 5 mm (¼ in) thick, and keep at room temperature. Blanch the snake beans for 30 seconds then refresh in iced water. Store at room temperature.

To Serve: Heat the clarified butter in a frying pan until bubbling, and fry the potatoes until they turn golden brown. Mix the snake beans with the fried potatoes, toss with olive oil and season with salt and pepper.

Preheat a griddle plate or barbecue to its hottest temperature – you will need it to be almost white-hot. Brush the slices of chilled ox tongue with a little olive oil and sear very quickly on each side (about 30 seconds) until they just colour. Drain on absorbent paper.

Arrange the potato and bean salad in the centre of each plate. Top with 3–4 slices of the seared ox tongue and drizzle over a little sticky mustard seed dressing.

Note: Please ask your butcher for a tongue that has been pickled for a minimum of 5 days.

Serves 6

slow-cooked lamb shanks
with creamed white beans, gremolata and watercress salad

**Slow-cooked
Lamb Shanks**

30 ml (1 fl oz)
pure olive oil

6 lamb shanks

sea salt

freshly ground
black pepper

3 litres (5¾ pints)
veal stock
(see Basics)

**Creamed
White Beans**

200 g (7 oz) white
haricot beans, soaked
overnight in water

100 ml (3½ fl oz)
thickened cream

sea salt

Aioli

½ bulb garlic

1 egg yolk

1 tablespoon
white wine vinegar

1 tablespoon
Dijon mustard

200 ml (7 fl oz)
pure olive oil

salt and pepper

Sauce

2 litres (4 pints)
reserved lamb
braising liquid

50 ml (1½ fl oz)
thickened cream

salt and pepper

Watercress Salad

3 medium vine-
ripened tomatoes

sea salt

½ cup watercress

Gremolata

1 lemon

½ cup parsley leaves,
finely chopped

½ cup mint leaves,
finely chopped

¼ cup basil leaves,
finely chopped

Slow-cooked Lamb Shanks: Preheat the oven to 180°C (350°F). Heat the olive oil in a large frying pan. Season the lamb shanks with salt and pepper and fry until nicely browned all over. Drain on absorbent paper. Transfer the lamb shanks to a deep braising dish. Bring the veal stock to the boil and pour over the shanks. Cover the dish with a lid or kitchen foil and braise for 2–3 hours until the meat is tender. Remove from the oven and allow the shanks to cool in the stock. When they are cold, remove the shanks from the braising liquid and refrigerate until ready to serve. Skim any fat from the braising liquid, strain it and reserve 2 litres for the sauce.

Creamed White Beans: Drain the soaked beans and rinse thoroughly. Place the beans in a medium saucepan and add enough fresh water to cover them by an inch. Bring the pan to the boil then lower the heat and simmer gently until tender, about half an hour. Drain the beans and allow them to steam dry for a few minutes. Tip them into a food processor, add the cream and purée until smooth. Season to taste and pass the bean purée through a sieve to remove the skins. Keep warm until ready to serve.

Aioli: Preheat the oven to 150°C (300°F). Wrap the garlic in a piece of lightly greased kitchen foil and roast until tender, about 30 minutes. Remove from the oven and allow to cool, then scrape the soft garlic away from the skins into a food processor. Add the egg yolk, white wine vinegar and mustard and purée until the mixture thickens and nearly doubles in size. Slowly add the oil until the mixture emulsifies and thickens. Season to taste and refrigerate until needed.

Sauce: Heat 2 litres (4 pints) of the reserved braising liquid in a small saucepan. Reduce by three-quarters while skimming away any impurities that rise to the surface. Add the cream and bring the sauce back to a gentle simmer. Reduce by a third again, then remove from the heat, season with salt and pepper and keep warm until ready to serve.

Watercress Salad: Preheat the oven to 150°C (300°F). Cut the tomatoes in half and remove the 'eye'. Place them on a baking tray lined with greaseproof paper. Sprinkle the tomatoes with salt and bake for 15–20 minutes until nicely browned. Wash and pick the watercress leaves.

Gremolata: Use a vegetable peeler to peel the skin from the lemon as thinly as possible. Try to avoid the pith, which tastes bitter. Finely chop the lemon skin and mix it with the herbs.

To Serve: Preheat the oven to 170°C (325°F). Place the lamb shanks in a deep braising dish and cover with the rest of the reserved braising liquid. Cover with foil and heat through very gently (if the oven temperature is too high the shanks will disintegrate). Gently reheat the white bean purée, stirring to prevent it burning.

Place a spoonful of the hot white bean purée in the centre of each bowl and smooth it around to form a neat circle, 5 cm (2 in) across. Carefully lift the lamb shanks out of the hot stock, one at a time. Coat each one with gremolata and sit in the centre of the plate criss-crossed. Place a generous dollop of aioli on one side of each plate and sit a tomato half on top of each shank. Carefully spoon a generous amount of sauce around the plate. Finish with a sprig of watercress.

Serves 6

sumac-spiced lamb cutlets
with sweet pomegranate, eggplant two ways
and a soft herb, persian fetta and lemon salad

Sumac-spiced Lamb

200 g (7 oz) caul fat

6 lamb racks,
four points each

60 g (2½ oz) sumac

Sweet Pomegranate Syrup

100 ml (3½ fl oz)
grenadine

200 g (7 oz) caster
(superfine) sugar

150 ml (5 fl oz) water

200 ml (7 fl oz)
pomegranate molasses

Soft Herb, Persian Fetta and Lemon Salad

1 cup marinated
Persian fetta

½ cup chervil sprigs

½ cup dill sprigs

1 cup chives, chopped
into 2 cm (¾ in) lengths

1 lemon, peel and pith
removed, finely diced

1 small red onion,
sliced into fine rings

Babaganoush

1 large eggplant
(aubergine)

3 cloves garlic,
crushed to a paste

3 tablespoons
tahini paste

juice of 1 lemons

salt

pepper

Eggplant Fritters

1 litre (1¾ pints)
vegetable oil for frying

1 eggplant (aubergine)

20 g (¾ oz) plain
(all-purpose) flour

300 ml (10½ fl oz)
beer batter
(see Basics)

This is yet another of my signature dishes. I like to think of it as a kind of Middle Eastern, sweet-and-sour lamb. Again, the success of the dish lies in the way the flavours are put together. Experiment a little until you achieve the balance of sweet-sour smokiness that works for you.

Sumac-Spiced Lamb: Lay the caul fat out on a work-surface and cut it into 6 pieces, each large enough to wrap around a lamb rack. Place a lamb rack in the centre of each piece of caul, fold in the ends and wrap into a neat parcel. Refrigerate until ready to cook.

Sweet Pomegranate Syrup: Place all the ingredients in a small non-reactive saucepan and bring to a gentle simmer. Reduce by half, brushing down the inside of the pan with water from time to time to stop it crystallising. Remove from the heat, allow to cool and store in a sealed container at room temperature.

Soft Herb, Persian Fetta and Lemon Salad: Prepare the salad ingredients and store separately in the fridge. When ready to serve, place all the ingredients in a large mixing bowl, and toss until well combined.

Babaganoush: Prick the eggplant all over with a fork and wrap tightly in kitchen foil. Sit the eggplant directly on a high flame on your stove, or place on a hot barbecue. Cook for about 4–6 minutes until the eggplants start to collapse. Remove from the heat, peel away the kitchen foil and place the eggplants in a colander, so the bitter juices can drain away. Carefully peel away all the skin from each eggplant and discard.

Place the garlic in a food processor with the tahini and blitz to a firm paste. Add a little hot water to loosen the paste, then add the eggplant, lemon juice, salt and pepper and blitz again to a coarse purée. Taste and adjust seasoning if needed.

Eggplant Fritters: Heat the oil in a medium-sized saucepan to 180ºC (350ºF). Slice the eggplant as thinly as possible into 12 discs (leave the skin on). Dust each slice of eggplant with flour, shaking off excess as you go, then dip in batter. Fry in small batches until golden brown, about 3–4 minutes, turning the fritters in the oil so they colour evenly. Remove from the oil and drain on absorbent paper.

To Serve: Preheat the oven to 200ºC (400ºF). Heat a large frying pan until nearly smoking. Place the lamb racks in the pan, meat side down, and sear until brown. Transfer the lamb racks to the hot oven and cook for 12–15 minutes. Remove from the oven and allow to rest in a warm place for 8 minutes. Roll each rack of lamb in sumac so that it is evenly coated, then slice into 3 even pieces.

Place a spoonful of babaganoush in the centre of each plate, and swirl some of the pomegranate syrup, followed by the pomegranate molasses, around the outside. Place the 3 pieces of lamb on top of the babaghanoush so that the bones point towards the outside of the plate. Top with an eggplant fritter and a small handful of salad. Finish with another fritter and serve immediately.

Serves 6

slow-cooked veal shanks
with soft truffle polenta, broad beans, mushrooms and fried jerusalem artichoke chips

Slow-cooked Veal Shanks

30 ml (1 fl oz) pure olive oil

6 large veal shanks, frenched (see Note)

sea salt

freshly ground black pepper

2.5 litres (5 pints) veal stock (see Basics)

Soft Truffle Polenta

250 ml (7 fl oz) milk

250 ml (7 fl oz) water

100 g (3½ oz) instant polenta

truffle oil to taste, about 3 drops

sea salt

freshly ground black pepper

1 tablespoon unsalted butter

1 tablespoon finely grated parmesan cheese

Broad Bean Sauce

500 ml (16 fl oz) veal stock, reserved after braising the veal

50 ml (1½ fl oz) thickened cream

100 g (3½ oz) button mushrooms

1 tablespoon butter

300 g (10 oz) broad beans, unshelled weight

sea salt

freshly ground black pepper

Fried Jerusalem Artichoke Chips

4 large Jerusalem artichokes

500 ml (16 fl oz) vegetable oil

sea salt

freshly ground black pepper

Slow-Cooked Veal Shanks: Preheat the oven to 160°C (325°F). Heat the olive oil in a large frying pan. Season the veal shanks with salt and pepper and fry until nicely browned all over. Drain on absorbent paper. Transfer the veal shanks to a deep braising dish. Bring the veal stock to the boil and pour over the shanks. Cover the dish with a lid or kitchen foil and braise for 2–3 hours until the meat is tender. Make sure the meat is completely covered. Remove from the oven and allow the shanks to cool in the stock. When they are cold, remove the shanks from the braising liquid and refrigerate until ready to serve. Skim any fat from the braising liquid, strain it and reserve.

Soft Truffle Polenta: Heat the milk and water in a medium-size saucepan. When it starts to simmer, pour in the polenta and whisk vigorously until it is all incorporated. Turn down the heat to a gentle simmer and cook for 6–7 minutes, stirring with a wooden spoon to stop the polenta sticking to the pan. When it comes away from the sides in a clean smooth mass remove from the heat and stir in the truffle oil. Season with salt and pepper and add the butter and parmesan. Cover tightly and keep warm until ready to serve.

Broad Bean Sauce: Heat 2 litres (4 pints) of the reserved braising liquid in a small saucepan. Reduce by three-quarters while skimming away any impurities that rise to the surface. Add the cream and bring the sauce back to a gentle simmer. Reduce by half again.

Cut the mushrooms into quarters. Sauté in small batches in butter in a dry frying pan until they are cooked and evenly coloured.

Pod the broad beans and blanch them for 20 seconds in a large pot of boiling water. Refresh in iced water then drain them well and peel off the skins.

Add the mushrooms and broad beans to the sauce and season with salt and pepper. Keep warm until ready to serve.

Fried Jerusalem Artichoke Chips: Use a very sharp knife to peel the artichokes and slice them very finely. Heat the oil in a medium pot or deep-fryer to 180ºC (350ºF). Fry the artichokes in batches until golden brown, about 3 minutes, then drain well on absorbent paper. Season with salt and pepper.

To Serve: Preheat the oven to 170ºC (325ºF). Place the veal shanks in a deep braising dish and cover with the rest of the reserved braising liquid. Cover with foil and heat through very gently (if the oven temperature is too high the shanks will disintegrate).

Divide the warm polenta evenly between 6 deep bowls. Carefully lift the veal shanks out of the hot stock, one at a time, and sit upright next to the polenta. Spoon the sauce around the shanks, garnish with the Jerusalem artichoke chips and serve straight away.

Note: Ask your butcher to 'french' the veal shanks, that is, to scrape the bone very clean, right down to the meat.

Serves 6

desserts

blood orange and aperol sorbet stack

with crème fraîche and pistachio wafers

Blood Orange and Aperol Sorbet

600 ml (20 fl oz) blood orange juice

400 ml (14 fl oz) sugar syrup (see Basics)

1 tablespoon glucose

50 ml (1¾ fl oz) Aperol (or Campari)

Pistachio Wafers

150 g (5 oz) wafer mix (see Basics), at room temperature

1 tablespoon unsalted pistachios, roughly chopped

Garnish

200 ml (7 fl oz) crème fraîche

Blood Orange and Aperol Sorbet: Mix together the orange juice and sugar syrup then stir in the glucose until it dissolves completely. Stir in the Aperol then pour the mixture into an ice-cream machine. Churn for 15–20 minutes, or until frozen. Scrape the sorbet into a clean container and freeze until required.

Pistachio Wafers: Preheat the oven to 140°C (280°F). Line a large baking sheet with non-stick paper. Using a template (see Note) to form perfect circles, spread the wafer mix as thinly and evenly as possible. The mix should make 18 wafers. Sprinkle each wafer with chopped pistachios and bake for 3–4 minutes, or until they are golden brown. Allow the wafers to cool on the tray, then transfer them carefully to an airtight container. They can be made the day before and re-heated for 10–15 seconds in a hot oven to crisp them up just before serving.

Garnish: Tip the crème fraîche into a mixing bowl and stir gently to the consistency of soft or semi-whipped cream. Spoon it into a piping bag fitted with a small nozzle and refrigerate until ready to serve.

To Serve: Pipe a ziz-zag of crème fraîche onto each plate. Arrange a pistachio wafer in the centre. Use an ice-cream scoop to form a neat ball of sorbet and place it on top of the wafer. Top with another wafer and another ball of sorbet, then finish with a wafer.

Note: To make a template for the wafers, use a very sharp knife to cut an 8 cm circle from a flat piece of plastic, no more than 1.5 mm (¹⁄₁₆ in) thick – something like the lid of an ice-cream container is ideal. Cut a second 6 cm circle inside the larger one, to form a plastic hoop, to act as a template.

Serves 6

mango and lychee salad
with mint sorbet and raspberry-chilli jam

Mint Sorbet

1 bunch mint

700 ml (22 fl oz) skim milk

400 ml (14 fl oz) sugar syrup (see Basics)

1 tablespoon glucose

Raspberry-Chilli Jam

500 g (1 lb) frozen raspberries

250 g (9 oz) caster (superfine) sugar

250 ml (9 fl oz) water

4 red bird's eye chillies, finely chopped

Mango and Lychee Salad

2 large ripe mangoes

18 lychees

The flavours in this dessert are really quite extraordinary. The mango and lychee salad is sweet and luscious, while the raspberry-chilli jam is both spicy-hot and intensely sweet. The mint sorbet is delicate and really refreshes the palate. This dish is best made when both mangoes and lychees are in season.

Mint Sorbet: Chop the bunch of mint into three sections and place with the milk in a medium-size non-reactive saucepan. Bring to a simmer for 5 minutes, then remove from the heat, cool and allow to infuse overnight in the refrigerator. Strain the infused milk, and measure out 600 ml into a clean bowl. The mint will have absorbed some of the milk as it infuses, so top up with a little extra skimmed milk if necessary. Stir in the sugar syrup and glucose, then pour the mix into an ice-cream machine and churn until frozen. Tip the sorbet into a clean container and freeze until ready to serve.

Raspberry-Chilli Jam: Defrost the raspberries and drain off any excess water. Place the sugar, water and chillies into a wide, heavy-based, non-reactive saucepan. Bring to the boil and reduce by roughly half, until the syrup has nearly reached the caramel stage. Brush down the inside of the pan with water from time to time to stop it crystallising. Add the raspberries and cook for 10 minutes until it reaches a jam-like consistency. Remove from the heat, allow to cool and push through a fine sieve. The quantities given here make more jam than you will need for this dessert, but it keeps very well in a tightly sealed jar in the refrigerator.

Mango and Lychee Salad: Peel the mangoes and slice the flesh. Peel the lychees and remove the stones. Refrigerate the fruit separately until ready to serve.

To Serve: Arrange 4 slices of mango in the centre of each plate to form a neat little circle. Place a neat scoop of sorbet on top of the mango and drizzle the edge of the plate with raspberry-chilli jam. Arrange 3 lychees around the mango and serve straight away.

Serves 6

unusual flavour combinations

'Testing the boundaries' is a bit of a philosophy of mine! I can't bear to think that diners who come to my restaurant might go away bored – in fact I consider it almost my duty to give them an exciting, unusual and inspiring culinary experience.

I find that desserts offer a great medium for experimenting with ideas and flavour combinations. It doesn't mean that I just chuck things together for the sake of being shocking. There is always a well-thought-out plan going on in the background, and it usually involves applying a traditional idea in a brand-new area.

For instance, I really like the idea of combining intensely sweet flavours with hot spicy flavours. There's nothing new in that, it's done all the time in savoury dressings and relishes. But it isn't as common in sweet dishes. I decided to see what would happen if I made a sweet raspberry jam flavoured with hot chillies – and the result was sensational (see page 140).

Another great example is my Coconut, Chilli and Lime sorbet (see page 163). The hot-sour combination is a classic throughout South East Asia, as is coconut – and I was delighted to discover how well these ingredients worked together in a sweet iced sorbet.

And then there's one of my all-time favourite desserts, which I have to confess started out as a bit of a joke on some of my English chef-friends. A couple of years back, it seemed as if every other dish on their menus involved Jerusalem artichokes and truffle oil, so I decided to have a little fun and created a crème brulée flavoured with Jerusalem artichoke and truffle oil. It's not quite as bizarre as it sounds – the Jerusalem artichokes are lightly caramelised, which brings out their intrinsic sweet nuttiness, and the truffle oil works its own special magic. In the end, though, it looks as if the joke's on me – it's one of the most popular desserts on my restaurant menu.

pink grapefruit, coriander and gin sorbet

with citrus fruits and pistachio wafers

Pink Grapefruit, Coriander and Gin Sorbet

600 ml (20 fl oz) pink grapefruit juice

400 ml (14 fl oz) sugar syrup (see Basics)

1 tablespoon glucose

3 coriander (cilantro) roots, very finely chopped

50 ml (1½ fl oz) gin

Citrus Fruits Salad

1 orange

1 pink grapefruit

1 blood orange

1 lime

1 lemon

Pistachio Wafers

100 g (3½ oz) wafer mix (see Basics), at room temperature

1 tablespoon chopped unsalted pistachio nuts

Don't underestimate the impact of really tangy citrus fruits at their peak. They make a sensationally cleansing and refreshing end to any meal. Use any combination of citrus fruits that you can find – tangelos, pomelos and mandarins would all work really well in this dish.

Pink Grapefruit, Coriander and Gin Sorbet: Strain the grapefruit juice into a bowl and stir in the sugar syrup. Add the glucose and stir until completely dissolved. Stir in the finely chopped coriander and the gin, then pour the sorbet mixture into an ice-cream machine and churn until frozen. Tip into a clean container and freeze until ready to serve.

Citrus Fruits Salad: Peel the citrus fruits and use a sharp knife to slice each segment out of its casing. Remove all pips, combine the fruit and refrigerate until chilled.

Pistachio Wafers: Preheat the oven to 140°C (280°F). Line a large baking sheet with non-stick paper. Using a template (see Note) to form perfect circles, spread the wafer mix as thinly and evenly as possible. The mix should make 18 wafers. Sprinkle each wafer with chopped pistachios and bake for 3–4 minutes, or until they are golden brown. Allow the wafers to cool on the tray, then transfer them carefully to an airtight container. They can be made the day before and re-heated for 10–15 seconds in a hot oven to crisp them up just before serving.

To Serve: Divide the citrus fruit salad between 6 dessert bowls and top with a scoop of sorbet. Garnish with a wafer biscuit tucked into the top of the sorbet.

Note: To make a template for the wafers, use a very sharp knife to cut an 8 cm circle from a flat piece of plastic, no more than 1.5 mm (¹⁄₁₆ in) thick – something like the lid of an ice-cream container is ideal. Cut a second 6 cm circle inside the larger one, to form a plastic hoop, to act as a template.

Serves 6

honeycrunch ice-cream
with toasted gingerbread, cinnamon oil and sugar swirls

Cinnamon Oil

(Needs 24 hours)

3 cinnamon sticks

100 ml (3½ fl oz) olive oil

1 teaspoon icing (confectioners') sugar

Honeycomb

400 g (14 oz) caster (superfine) sugar

1 tablespoon glucose

125 ml (4 fl oz) water

1½ tablespoons bicarbonate of soda

Honeycrunch Ice-Cream

500 ml (16 fl oz) milk

500 ml (16 fl oz) thickened cream

160 g (5½ oz) honey

12 egg yolks

190 g (6½ oz) caster (superfine) sugar

Gingerbread

225 g (8 oz) plain (all-purpose) flour

½ teaspoon bicarbonate of soda

¼ teaspoon salt

¼ teaspoon ground ginger

¼ teaspoon allspice

150 g (5 oz) treacle

150 ml (5 fl oz) milk

80 g (3 oz) unsalted butter

1 egg yolk

Sugar Swirls

250 ml (9 fl oz) water

250 g (9 oz) caster (superfine) sugar

This is an ezard classic, and one that is always in demand. It combines favourite flavours such as sweet cinnamon and ginger with an irresistible honeycrunch ice-cream.

Cinnamon Oil: Preheat the oven to 180ºC (350ºF). Dry-roast the cinnamon sticks until fragrant, about 4–5 minutes. Remove from the oven and grind roughly with a mortar and pestle. Place the cinnamon in a small saucepan with the olive oil bring to a simmer. Remove from the heat and allow the oil to infuse for a minimum of 24 hours. Stir in the icing sugar and leave to stand until ready to use.

Honeycomb: Line a baking tray with non-stick paper. Mix the sugar, glucose and water in a small non-reactive saucepan and heat until the sugar dissolves. Bring to the boil, then simmer until the syrup starts to colour at the edges. Add the bicarbonate of soda and whisk in vigorously, then pour immediately into the prepared tray and allow to cool. When cold, break the honeycomb into bite-size pieces and store in an airtight container until needed. This quantity will be more than needed for the ice-cream, but any left over will keep extremely well in the freezer.

Honeycrunch Ice-Cream: Place the milk, cream and honey in a saucepan and bring to a simmer. In a separate bowl, whisk together the eggs and sugar until they and become thick and pale. Pour on the hot milk mixture and whisk vigorously. Place the bowl over a saucepan of simmering water. Heat gently for 5–10 minutes, stirring all the time, until the custard thickens enough to coat the back of a spoon. Place the bowl in a sink of iced water and allow to cool. Tip the custard into an ice-cream machine and churn until frozen. Stir in the pieces of honeycomb then tip the ice-cream into a clean container and place in the freezer until ready to serve.

Gingerbread: Preheat the oven to 180°C (350°F). Grease a standard loaf tin and line with non-stick paper. Place all the dry ingredients in a large bowl and stir to combine.

Put the treacle, milk and butter in a saucepan and heat until the butter melts. Pour onto the dry ingredients and stir well with a wooden spoon, then add the egg yolk and mix well. Tip the gingerbread mixture into the prepared loaf tin and bake for 30–40 minutes, or until the cake tests clean. Cool the gingerbread on a wire rack before turning out.

To toast the gingerbread, preheat the oven to 180°C (350°F). Cut the cake into 18 slices, about 2 mm ($\frac{1}{10}$ in) thick. Use a 5 cm (2 in) cookie-cutter to cut a circle from each slice and arrange on a baking sheet. Toast for 2–3 minutes, taking care not to let the gingerbread burn. When cool, transfer the toasted gingerbread to an airtight container until needed.

Sugar Swirls: Mix the water and sugar in a small non-reactive saucepan and heat until the sugar dissolves. Simmer gently until the syrup starts to colour and turn to caramel. Watch very carefully, and when the caramel is a medium-brown remove from the heat and allow to cool for 5 minutes. Lay a sheet of non-stick paper on a work surface and drizzle the caramel on, making spirals about 10 cm (4 in) wide. Allow the sugar swirls to set hard and keep until ready to serve.

To Serve: Drizzle a little cinnamon oil onto the base of each dessert bowl. Place a piece of toasted gingerbread in each bowl and top with a scoop of ice-cream. Repeat with another piece of gingerbread and another scoop of ice-cream and finish with a sugar swirl. Scatter a few pieces of honeycomb around the bowl.

Serves 6

espresso ice-cream
with sambucca jelly shot and hazelnut biscotti

Espresso Ice-Cream	Sambucca Jelly Shot	Hazelnut Biscotti
500 ml (16 fl oz) milk	250 ml (9 fl oz) water	125 g (4½ oz) hazelnuts
500 ml (16 fl oz) thickened cream	150 g (5 oz) caster (superfine) sugar	3 egg whites
2 cups whole coffee beans, lightly bruised with a rolling pin	2 gelatine leaves	225 g (8 oz) caster (superfine) sugar
	50 ml (1½ fl oz) Sambucca	250 g (9 oz) plain (all-purpose) flour
12 egg yolks		½ teaspoon bicarbonate of soda
250 g (9 oz) caster (superfine) sugar		2 teaspoons strong black coffee

Every one loves jelly and ice-cream, so you could describe this as the perfect dessert for big kids (aged 18 and over). The sophisticated combination of aniseed sambucca with strong dark coffee is incredibly popular, which might account for why this dish is so popular at the restaurant.

Espresso Ice-Cream: Place the milk, cream and coffee beans in a medium saucepan and bring to a very gentle simmer. Remove from heat and leave to infuse for around 20 minutes.

Whisk the egg yolks and sugar in a mixing bowl until they turn pale and start to thicken. Strain the hot coffee infusion onto the egg yolks, whisking briskly. Place the bowl over a pan of simmering water and cook, stirring constantly, until the mixture thickens enough to coat the back of a spoon. Remove the bowl from the heat and plunge into a sink of iced water to stop the custard cooking. When the custard is cold, pour it into an ice-cream machine and churn until frozen. Tip into a clean container and store in the freezer.

Sambucca Jelly Shot: Soak the gelatine leaves in cold water to soften, then squeeze out excess water. Mix the water and sugar in a small non-reactive saucepan and heat gently until the sugar dissolves completely. Remove from the heat. In another small saucepan, heat a tablespoon of water, add the gelatine to this and stir until it dissolves and there are no lumps. Pour on the sugar syrup and mix well. Stir in the Sambucca, pour into a shallow container and place in the fridge to set.

Hazelnut Biscotti: Preheat the oven to 180ºC (350ºF). Roast the hazelnuts for about 5 minutes, until the skins start to loosen. Tip them into a tea towel and briskly rub away the skins. Chop the nuts roughly.

Preheat the oven to 160ºC (325ºF). Grease a small loaf tin and line it with non-stick paper. Whisk the egg whites until they start to foam. Add the sugar and whisk until the mixture forms soft peaks. Fold in the chopped hazelnuts, flour and bicarbonate of soda. Finally fold through the black coffee.

Pour the biscotti mixture into the prepared tin and bake for 25–30 minutes or until golden brown and firm to touch. Cool in the tin. When cold use a serrated knife to slice off the outer crust, then cut carefully lengthwise into slices about 2 mm (1/10 in) thick. Cut each long slice in half diagonally to form triangles. Turn the oven temperature up to 180ºC (350ºF). Arrange the biscotti slices on a baking tray and return to the oven until crispy, 4–5 minutes. Remove from the oven and cool completely before storing in an airtight tin.

To Serve: Place a scoop of ice-cream on the centre of each plate. Fill each shot glass with jelly and place in bowls next to the ice-cream. Stick two biscotti, pointing upwards, into each scoop of ice-cream. Accompany with chocolate-covered coffee beans (optional).

Serves 6

infusing

In the same way that we use wet spice pastes in savoury dishes to build intense layers of complex flavours into a dish, I like to use infusions of spices and other aromatics to build layers of flavour in desserts.

The process typically involves roasting dried aromatics and spices to bring out their flavour and then infusing them for anything up to 24 hours in milk, cream or oil. The result is actually much more refined than what you achieve with a wet spice paste, so is quite appropriate for a dessert.

Some of my favourite infusions are toasted coconut, cinnamon sticks, nutmeg, cloves, star anise and dried mandarin peel.

The added bonus from infusions is that they add very little colour to a dish. I love the surprise that you see in people's eyes when they bite into a creamy-white pannacotta, for instance, and find it to be intensely flavoured. It's another way of adding an element of excitement to a dish.

mascarpone parfait
with fresh figs and sticky vanilla syrup

Mascarpone Parfait

3 eggs

105 g (3½ oz) caster
(superfine) sugar

220 g (8 oz)
mascarpone,
at room temperature

3 egg whites

Sticky Vanilla Syrup

200 g (7 oz) caster
(superfine) sugar

150 ml (5 fl oz) water

2 vanilla beans,
split and scraped

6 large black figs

Mascarpone and figs is a classic combination equally well suited to savoury and sweet dishes. This parfait is really rich and creamy, and brings out the luscious sweetness of perfectly ripe black figs. The slight spiciness in the vanilla syrup really brings the dish together.

Mascarpone Parfait: Lightly oil individual dariole moulds. Mix the whole eggs and 75 g (3 oz) of the sugar together in a medium-size bowl. Place over a saucepan of simmering water and whisk until the mixture becomes thick and pale, about 5 minutes. Remove from the heat and continue to whisk as it cools. When the sabayon is cold, its consistency should be similar to that of the mascarpone. Gently fold the mascarpone into the sabayon. Whisk the egg whites with the remaining sugar until they form soft peaks, and fold into the sabayon mixture. Pour the parfait mixture into the prepared dariole moulds and freeze.

Sticky Vanilla Syrup: Mix the sugar and water in a small non-reactive saucepan until the sugar dissolves and the syrup boils. Lower the heat and simmer gently for 10–15 minutes until the syrup is reduced by half. Remove from the heat and allow to cool slightly. Add the vanilla seeds to the syrup and stir well. Pour the syrup into a clean container and keep until ready to serve.

To Serve: Drizzle a generous spoonful of vanilla syrup around each plate. Cut each fig into thin slices crosswise, and arrange on each plate. Unmould the parfaits and arrange them on top of the figs and drizzle with a little extra syrup.

Serves 6

five-spiced pannacotta
with poached pears and dark palm sugar syrup

Five-spiced Pannacotta	Poached Pears	Dark Palm Sugar Syrup	Garnish
2 cinnamon sticks	3 pears	200 g (7 oz) dark palm sugar, roughly chopped	½ cup Persian fairy floss
4 star anise	200 g (7 oz) dark palm sugar, roughly chopped	200 ml (7 fl oz) water	
6 cardamom pods	300 ml (10½ fl oz) water	1 cinnamon stick	
2 nutmegs	zest of 1 orange	3 star anise	
3 cloves	1 cinnamon stick	3 cardamom pods	
300 ml (10½ fl oz) full cream milk	3 star anise	peel of 1 mandarin	
300 ml (10½ fl oz) thickened cream			
3 leaves gelatine			
70 g (2½ oz) caster (superfine) sugar			
1 tablespoon honey			

This is a dish that really excites and intrigues the palate. I love the way a pale, creamy-smooth panacotta can have such surprisingly intense and aromatic flavours. The Asian inspiration is carried further by the deep, almost treacly sweetness of the dark palm sugar syrup. At the restaurant we serve this dessert in Chinese bowls, which suits it perfectly.

Pannacotta: Preheat the oven to 180ºC (350ºF). Arrange the cinnamon, star anise, cardamom, nutmeg and cloves on a small oven tray and roast for 4–5 minutes, until fragrant. Place the roasted spices in a clean tea towel and crush them roughly with a rolling pin. Put the bruised spices in a small saucepan with the milk and simmer very gently for 10 minutes to infuse, but be careful not to let the milk boil. Remove from the heat and allow to stand – preferably overnight for the maximum intensity of flavour.

Whip the cream until it forms soft peaks. Soak the gelatine in cold water for about a minute until it softens, then squeeze out any excess water. Place the sugar and honey in a saucepan with the softened gelatine, pour on the infused milk and heat gently until everything dissolves. Strain the warm milk into a clean saucepan through a fine sieve and place in a sink of iced water to chill. Stir constantly until the mixture is on the verge of setting, then fold in the whipped cream. Pour the mixture into 6 oiled dariole moulds or ramekin dishes and refrigerate until set.

Poached Pears: Peel the pears, then cut them into quarters and remove the cores. Place them in acidulated water to stop them discolouring while you prepare the poaching syrup. Place the palm sugar, water, orange zest and spices in a medium-size pan and bring to the boil. Add the pears to the syrup and simmer gently until they are tender – this will vary according to the variety and ripeness of the pears. Once cooked, leave to cool in the syrup.

Dark Palm Sugar Syrup: Place all the ingredients in a non-reactive saucepan and bring to the boil. Lower the heat and simmer until the syrup is reduced by two-thirds, and is the consistency of runny honey. From time to time you will need to skim away any scum that rises to the surface. Remove from the heat and strain the syrup into a clean container. Once cool, refrigerate until ready to serve.

To Serve: Carefully unmould the pannacottas into 6 chilled dessert bowls. Remove the pears from their poaching syrup and cut each quarter into 4 slices. Arrange the slices around the pannacotta then drizzle with palm sugar syrup and garnish with a pinch of Persian fairy floss.

Serves 6

crème brulée
flavoured with jerusalem artichoke and white truffle oil

Crème Brulée

(Needs 24 hours)

500 g (16 oz) Jerusalem artichokes

2 tablespoons unsalted butter

2 tablespoons caster (superfine) sugar

2 vanilla beans, split and scraped

100 ml (3½ fl oz) milk

8 egg yolks

120 g (4½ oz) caster (superfine) sugar

250 ml (9 fl oz) thickened cream

250 ml (9 fl oz) pure cream

few drops white truffle oil to taste

½ cup demerara sugar

Garnish

1 Jerusalem artichoke

1 teaspoon pure icing (confectioners') sugar

This dessert is pretty wild. It says a lot about what you can – or should I say cannot – do with food, and has created a tremendous amount of interest. I like the earthy and nutty flavour of Jerusalem artichokes, and when they are cooked and caramelised they take on another dimension altogether. The aromatic truffle oil and spicy sweet vanilla ensure it is a triumph in my repertoire.

Crème Brulée: Peel and roughly slice the artichokes. In a medium-sized, heavy-based, non-reactive frying pan, melt the butter until it starts to bubble. Add the artichokes to the pan and toss them over the heat until lightly browned. Add the sugar and vanilla bean and cook for around 10 minutes until the mixture turns a deep golden caramel. Don't hurry this part of the dish – it is important to get as much colour and caramel flavour as possible from the artichokes. Add the milk, bring to a gentle simmer and cook the artichokes for 20 minutes. Remove from the heat and leave the mixture to infuse for half an hour before straining through a piece of muslin.

In a large bowl mix together the egg yolks and caster sugar until the sugar dissolves. Put the thickened cream and pure cream in a saucepan with the infused milk and bring to a gentle simmer. Pour onto the eggs and sugar and whisk well. Stir in the truffle oil to taste (about ½ teaspoon).

Preheat the oven to 150°C (300°F). Place 6 small soufflé dishes or ramekins in a deep baking tray lined with a tea towel – this stops the dishes moving around while cooking. Fill each soufflé dish up to the brim with the brulée mix. Pour hot water into the baking tray to come between halfway and two-thirds of the way up the sides of the soufflé dishes. Cover the tray loosely with a sheet of foil and place in the oven to bake for 20 minutes, or until the brulées are just set. Allow them to cool and refrigerate until ready to serve.

Garnish: Preheat the oven to 60°C (140°F). Peel the artichoke and use a mandolin or very sharp knife to slice it into fine wafers. Lay the wafers on a baking sheet lined with non-stick paper and place in the oven overnight (or for around 6 hours) to dry. Once the artichoke wafers are crisp, remove them from the oven to cool, then store in an airtight container.

To Serve: Preheat your griller to its highest temperature. Remove the crème brulées from the fridge and sprinkle each one evenly with demerara sugar. Place them under the grill for a few moments until the sugar caramelises, then leave them to cool and the sugar to set hard. If you have a domestic blowtorch, this is even more effective.

Dust the crispy artichoke wafers with icing sugar. Place each brulée on small plate and serve topped with 3 artichoke wafers.

Serves 6

five-spiced crème brulée
with spicy sugar and oven-dried pear crackers

Crème Brulée

2 cinnamon sticks

6 star anise

2 cardamom pods

2 nutmegs

2 cloves

100 ml (3½ fl oz) milk

8 egg yolks

120 g (4½ fl oz) caster (superfine) sugar

250 ml (9 fl oz) thickened cream

250 ml (9 fl oz) pure cream

½ cup demerara sugar

Spicy Sugar

2 tablespoons ground cinnamon

6 tablespoons icing (confectioners') sugar

Pear Crackers

1 large pear

Crème Brulée: Preheat the oven to 180°C (350°F). Arrange the cinnamon, star anise, cardamom, nutmeg and cloves on a small oven tray and roast for 4–5 minutes, until fragrant. Place the roasted spices in a clean tea towel and crush them roughly with a rolling pin. Put the bruised spices in a small saucepan with the milk and simmer very gently for 10 minutes to infuse, but be careful not to let the milk boil. Remove from the heat and allow to cool.

In a large bowl mix together the egg yolks and caster sugar until the sugar dissolves. Put the thickened cream and pure cream in a saucepan with the infused milk and bring to a gentle simmer. Pour onto the eggs and sugar and whisk well.

Preheat the oven to 160°C (325°F). Place 6 soufflé or ramekin dishes, about 10 cm (4 in) wide, in a deep baking tray lined with a tea towel – this stops the dishes moving around while cooking. Fill each soufflé dish up to the brim with the brulée mix. Pour hot water into the baking tray to come between halfway and two-thirds of the way up the sides of the soufflé dishes. Cover the tray loosely with a sheet of foil and place in the oven to bake for 20–30 minutes until the brulées are just set. Allow them to cool and refrigerate until ready to serve.

Spicy Sugar: Sieve the cinnamon and icing (confectioners') sugar together into a bowl. Mix well to combine then store in an airtight container until ready to serve.

Pear Crackers: Preheat the oven to 80°C (175°F). Trim off both ends of the pear and use a mandolin or very sharp knife to slice the pear crosswise, as thinly as possible. Lay the pear slices on a baking sheet lined with non-stick paper and place in the oven overnight (or for around 6 hours) to dry. Once the pear slices are crisp, remove them from the oven to cool, then store in an airtight container.

To Serve: Preheat your griller to its highest temperature. Remove the crème brulées from the fridge and sprinkle each one evenly with sugar. Place them under the grill for a few moments until the sugar caramelises, then leave them to cool and the sugar to set hard. If you have a domestic blowtorch, this is even more effective.

Dust the pear crackers with spicy sugar. Place each brulée on small plate and serve topped with 3 pear crackers.

Serves 6

crispy honeyed-filo stack

with passionfruit curd, citrus fruits, pistachio nuts and rosewater-pomegranate syrup

Crispy Honeyed-Filo

1 x 375 g (13 oz) packet of filo pastry

125 ml (4½ fl oz) clarified butter

1 tablespoon honey

100 g (3½ oz) icing (confectioners') sugar

Passionfruit Curd

10 egg yolks

200 g (7 oz) caster (superfine) sugar

600 ml (20 fl oz) fresh passionfruit juice (from about 1 kg (2 lb) of whole passionfruit)

200 g (7 oz) chilled unsalted butter, diced

Citrus Fruits

2 pink grapefruit

2 oranges

1 lemon

Rosewater-Pomegranate Syrup

100 ml (3½ fl oz) pomegranate juice (juice from about 2 ripe pomegranates)

1 teaspoon rosewater

Garnish

1 tablespoon unsalted pistachio nuts

I love Middle Eastern flavours, and this dessert includes two of my favourites: rosewater and pomegranate. I call it romance on a plate, with the sweet honeyed filo, slightly tart passionfruit and citrus, and crunchy pistachios, all drawn together by the fragrant syrup. Unfortunately pomegranates have a very short season, so be sure to buy them as soon as they hit the markets.

Crispy Honeyed-Filo: Preheat the oven to 180°C (350°F). Remove the filo from its packet and unroll so it lies flat. Keep the pastry covered with a damp cloth while you work to prevent it from drying out. Warm the clarified butter.

On a clean work surface lie 2 sheets of filo out, side by side, and brush each one lightly with the clarified butter. Top each sheet with 4 more pastry layers, brushing each with butter as you go. Use a 6 cm (2½ in) pastry cutter to cut 24 circles from the pastry and place them onto baking sheets lined with non-stick paper. Bake for around 5 minutes, until golden brown. Drizzle a little warm honey over each pastry circle and bake for a further minute. Transfer to a wire rack and allow to cool.

Passionfruit Curd: In a medium-size bowl, whisk together the egg yolks and caster sugar until light and creamy. Place the bowl over a pan of simmering water and add the passionfruit juice, then stir until the mixture thickens. Add the butter, one piece at a time, making sure that each is thoroughly incorporated before adding the next. Stir continuously until the mixture is thick. Remove from the heat and cool over a bowl of iced water. Refrigerate until ready to serve.

Citrus Fruits: Peel the citrus fruits and use a sharp knife to slice each segment out of its casing. Remove all pips, combine the fruit and refrigerate.

Rosewater-Pomegranate Syrup: Mix together the pomegranate juice and rosewater and reserve until ready to serve.

Garnish: Preheat the oven to 160°C (325°F). Roast the pistachio nuts for a few minutes until their skins start to loosen. Tip them into a clean tea towel and rub the skins away completely. Chop the pistachios roughly and store in an airtight container until needed.

To Serve: Lightly dust the filo pastry discs with icing sugar. Place one on the centre of each plate and top with a spoonful of chilled citrus fruits and a spoonful of passionfruit curd. Top with two more layers of pastry, fruit and curd, finishing with a pastry layer. Garnish with chopped pistachios and drizzle the rosewater-pomegranate syrup around the plate.

Serves 6

chocolate tart
with raspberry caramel

Chocolate Tart Filling

140 g (5 oz)
Callebaut chocolate,
roughly chopped

130 g (4½ oz) unsalted
butter, roughly chopped

5 eggs

225 g (8 oz) caster
(superfine) sugar

70 g (3 oz) plain
(all-purpose) flour,
sifted

Raspberry Caramel

250 g (9 oz) caster
(superfine) sugar

150 ml (5 fl oz) water

250 g (9 oz) fresh or
frozen raspberries

Sweet Pastry

125 g (4½ oz)
unsalted butter

125 g (4½ oz)
icing (confectioners')
sugar

1 vanilla bean

1 egg

250 g (9 oz)
plain (all-purpose)
flour, sifted

pinch of salt

Garnish

250 ml (9 fl oz)
pure cream

I doubt there are more than a handful of restaurants in the Western world that don't have at least one chocolate dessert on their menus. This is one of my favourites, with the rich and luscious chocolate filling contrasting brilliantly with the slight tartness of raspberries. Although you could cheat and buy ready-made pastry, it's worth taking the time to make your own – this dessert deserves the best!

Chocolate Tart Filling: Combine the chocolate and butter in a bowl over a pan of simmering water or in a double boiler. Stir until the mixture has melted to a smooth consistency.

In another bowl or double boiler, whisk together the eggs and sugar until the mixture thickens to a pale creamy sabayon. Add the chocolate to the sabayon and stir through to combine thoroughly. Gently fold in the sifted flour then pour the mixture into a clean container and allow to cool.

Raspberry Caramel: Defrost and drain the rasberries of all liquid if frozen. Stir the sugar and water in a saucepan and heat gently until the sugar dissolves. Cook until the syrup colours and starts to caramelise. Add the raspberries and cook for a few minutes until the raspberries start to break down. Remove from the heat and allow to cool a little. Purée until smooth, and strain through a sieve to remove the seeds.

Sweet Pastry: Place the butter and sugar in an electric mixer and cream until smooth. Split the vanilla bean in half lengthwise and scrape out the seeds with the tip of a knife. Add the vanilla seeds to the creamed mixture and mix in well. Add the egg and combine well, and then the flour and salt. Mix until the pastry comes together as a ball. Tip it out of the mixer and mix – do not knead – the pastry by hand for a few minutes until it is smooth. Wrap in plastic wrap and refrigerate for half an hour.

Preheat the oven to 160°C (325°F). Lay the pastry on a floured work surface. Use your hands to roll the pastry into a sausage and cut into 6 even pieces. Next, use a rolling pin to roll each piece of pastry into a circle about 2 mm (⅛ in) thick. Lift each piece of pastry onto a well-greased 9 cm (3½ in) tart ring and blind-bake for 10–12 minutes, or until the pastry is golden brown. Remove from the oven and allow the pastry shells to cool in the tart rings.

To Serve: Preheat the oven to 180°C (350°F). Divide the chocolate mixture between the 6 tart shells and bake for around 8 minutes, or until just set. Remove the tarts from the oven and allow them to cool slightly before serving – the filling should be slightly fudgy in the middle.

Spoon the raspberry caramel onto each plate and carefully remove each tart from its ring and place a tart on top. Finish with a generous dollop of cream.

Serves 6

poached quince tarts
with star anise ice-cream and honey snap wafers

Poached Quinces

3 large quinces

2 cinnamon sticks

3 star anise

300 g (10 oz) caster (superfine) sugar

500 ml (16 fl oz) water

zest of 1 orange

Pastry Cream

350 ml (12 fl oz) milk

150 ml (5 fl oz) thickened cream

1 vanilla bean

75 g (3 oz) caster (superfine) sugar

1 egg

3 egg yolks

40 g (1½ oz) cornflour (cornstarch)

Sweet Pastry

125 g (4½ oz) unsalted butter, softened

125 g (4½ oz) caster (superfine) sugar

1 vanilla bean

1 egg

250 g (9 oz) plain (all-purpose) flour

pinch of salt

Star Anise Ice-Cream

½ cup star anise

500 ml (16 fl oz) milk

500 ml (16 fl oz) cream

12 egg yolks

250 g (7 oz) caster (superfine) sugar

Honey Snap Wafers

50 g (1¾ oz) plain (all-purpose) flour, sifted

50 g (1¾ oz) caster (superfine) sugar

50 g (1¾ oz) honey

50 g (1¾ oz) unsalted butter, softened

The secret to poaching quinces is time – simply be patient, and eventually you will be rewarded with tender, fragrant, gloriously pink fruit. While the quinces are cooking prepare the other components of this beautiful winter dish. Of course, the star anise ice-cream is popular all year round, and teams well with summer fruits like pineapple or sweet, ripe nectarines. Add a honey snap wafer for some crunch.

Poached Quinces: Peel the quinces and cut them into quarters. Cut away the cores and place the quince pieces in acidulated water to prevent discolouration. Collect all the peelings and seeds and put them into a piece of muslin with the cinnamon and star anise. Tie the cloth into a ball with string. Put the sugar, water and orange zest in a medium-size non-reactive saucepan. Bring it to a simmer then add the spice bag and quinces. Poach gently until the quinces are tender. When cooked, remove the pan from the heat and allow the quinces to cool in the poaching syrup.

Pastry Cream: Put the milk, cream and vanilla bean in a small heavy-based saucepan and bring to the boil. In a separate bowl, beat the eggs, egg yolks and the sugar until pale and thick. Sift the cornflour into the eggs and stir in well. Pour on a quarter of the boiling milk and whisk until smooth. Tip the mixture back into the hot milk and cook gently for 4–5 minutes, stirring continuously to avoid lumps. When cooked the pastry cream will be smooth, thick and shiny. Remove the vanilla bean and pour the pastry cream into a clean container. Press plastic wrap onto the surface of the cream to prevent a skin forming and refrigerate.

Sweet Pastry: Place the butter and sugar in an electric mixer and cream until smooth. Split the vanilla bean in half lengthwise and scrape out the seeds with the tip of a knife. Add the vanilla seeds to the creamed mixture and mix in well. Add the egg and combine well, and then the flour and salt. Mix until the pastry comes together as a ball. Tip it out of the mixer and wrap in plastic wrap and refrigerate for half an hour.

Preheat the oven to 160°C (325°F). Lay the pastry on a floured work surface. Use your hands to roll the pastry into a sausage and cut into 6 even pieces. Next, use a rolling pin to roll each piece of pastry into a circle about 1.5 mm–2 mm (less than ¹⁄₁₀ in) thick. Lift each piece of pastry onto a well-greased 9 cm (3½ in) tart ring and blind-bake for 10–12 minutes, or until the pastry is golden brown. Remove from the oven and allow the pastry shells to cool in the tart rings.

Star Anise Ice-Cream: Preheat the oven to 200ºC (400ºF). Roast the star anise for 3–4 minutes until fragrant, then grind roughly using a mortar and pestle. Put the spices in a small saucepan with the milk and cream and infuse over a very low heat for 10 minutes. Remove from the heat and allow to infuse for another half-hour. Whisk the egg yolks and sugar in a mixing bowl until they turn pale and start to thicken. Bring the milk back to the boil and strain onto the egg yolks, whisking briskly. Place the bowl over a pan of simmering water and cook, stirring constantly, until the mixture thickens enough to coat the back of a spoon. Remove the bowl from the heat and plunge into a sink of iced water to stop the custard cooking. When the custard is cold, pour it into an ice-cream machine and churn until frozen. Tip into a clean container and store in the freezer.

Honey Snap Wafers: Preheat the oven to 140ºC (275ºF) and line a baking sheet with non-stick paper. Place all the ingredients into a food processor and blitz until smooth. Scrape the mixture onto a clean work surface, wrap in plastic wrap and chill briefly until it firms. Divide the mixture into 6 and roll into little balls, about the size of a thumbnail. Place them onto the prepared baking sheet, about 10 cm (4 in) apart, and cook for 5–10 minutes until they start to bubble and turn golden brown. Allow the biscuits to cool on the tray, and transfer to an airtight container.

To Serve: To assemble the tarts, carefully remove each pastry shell from its ring and half fill with pastry cream. Trim the quince quarters to the same size as the tart (about 9 cm / 3½ in), cut each quarter into 4 slices and arrange them on top of the tarts. Carefully place a tart onto each dessert plate and top with a scoop of ice-cream. Serve garnished with a honey snap biscuit.

Serves 6

coconut

I love coconut. In fact I really, really love coconut – in the restaurant we get through loads of fresh coconuts every week and I use them in all kinds of savoury and sweet dishes. And as just about every country in South East Asia loves coconut too (except, as far as I know, Vietnam) I guess I'm not alone.

Many Asian cuisines like to use nuts and grains in wet spice mixes to add texture and a sweet flavour point. Typically, they will be peanuts, candlenuts, cashew nuts and coconuts. Of them all, coconut is my favourite – probably as a result of my culinary adventures travelling through Indonesia, which is where I learnt everything I ever wanted to know about coconuts – and more.

The flesh of young coconuts is delicious cut into fine slivers for salads or finely grated and added to all kinds of savoury and sweet dishes. But it is for coconut milk that the nut is most used. Coconut milk is not the watery liquid inside a coconut, but is the liquid extracted from the grated flesh. While you can buy coconut milk and coconut cream very readily in cans, the fresh version is far superior with a delicate fragrance and sweet nutty flavour.

I must be honest, making coconut milk is labour intensive and hard work. I use a method that I learnt in Bali, which involves lightly toasting the coconut first, as I find this intensifies the nutty flavour (see page 9 for a detailed explanation of the technique). The finely grated flesh is then soaked in an equal amount of water and squeezed to extract as much liquid as possible. This is 'first squeeze' coconut milk. The process can then be repeated as many as three times, but each subsequent 'squeeze' is thinner and less flavoursome.

Occasionally my recipes call for coconut cream, which you can buy in tins or in hard blocks – but always choose one that is unsweetened. Coconut cream is richer and slightly sweeter than coconut milk and adds a thicker, creamier texture to a dish.

The key thing to remember when using coconut cream is that if you add it straight to a hot pan to cook, it will split and curdle. What you need to do is boil a little bit of the cream on its own for a few minutes first – you will soon see the coconut split into oil and solids. Then you can add the remaining cream and it will emulsify without the risk of splitting again.

green coconut pancakes
with dark palm sugar syrup and coconut, chilli and lime sorbet

Green Coconut Pancakes

60 g (2 oz) plain (all-purpose) flour

1 teaspoon caster (superfine) sugar

1 egg

350 ml (11½ fl oz) coconut milk

½ teaspoon pandan leaf essence

1 teaspoon unsalted butter

Pancake Filling

2 cups grated, toasted coconut (see Toasted Coconut Milk in Basics)

4 tablespoons gula melaka syrup (see Basics)

juice of 2 limes

Dark Palm Sugar Syrup

200 g (7 oz) dark palm sugar

200 ml (7 fl oz) water

1 cinnamon stick

3 star anise

3 cardamom pods

Coconut, Chilli and Lime Sorbet

500 ml (16 fl oz) toasted coconut milk (see Basics)

750 ml (1½ pints) sugar syrup (see Basics)

3 teaspoons glucose

1 red Lombok chilli, seeded and finely chopped

3 fresh kaffir lime leaves, (or 3 teaspoons lime zest), finely chopped

30 ml (1 fl oz) Malibu

I must be honest: making this dessert is a labour of love. Grating fresh coconuts for the filling and making coconut milk are both very time-consuming – needless to say I wouldn't include the recipe if I didn't think the result was worth the effort. Try it and you'll see what I mean!

Green Coconut Pancakes: Put the flour and sugar into a mixing bowl and mix together. Gradually whisk in the egg and coconut milk until you get a smooth lump-free batter. Stir in the pandan leaf essence and refrigerate for a good hour before cooking.

Heat a medium-size non-stick frying pan or crêpe pan. Melt the butter and wipe it around the pan. Ladle in some batter and swirl to spread it to the edges of the pan (tip any excess back into the bowl). Cook the pancake until small bubbles begin to appear on the surface, 1–2 minutes. Use a spatula to turn the pancake over carefully and cook the other side for another minute or so. Transfer the cooked pancake onto a piece of non-stick paper and continue until the batter is used up – there should be sufficient quantity to make at least 6 pancakes.

Pancake Filling: Put the toasted coconut, gula melaka and lime juice in a mixing bowl and stir together well. Only add enough moisture to moisten the coconut. The consistency will be porridge-like with a sweet and slightly sour flavour. It is important that the gula melaka be quite thick or the filling will be too thin and watery.

Dark Palm Sugar Syrup: Place all the ingredients in a non-reactive saucepan and bring to the boil. Lower the heat and simmer until reduced by three-quarters. Allow to cool – the consistency should then be similar to honey. From time to time you will need to skim away any scum that rises to the surface. Remove from the heat and strain the syrup into a clean container. Once cool, refrigerate until ready to serve.

Coconut, Chilli and Lime Sorbet: Mix together the toasted coconut milk, sugar syrup and glucose. Stir well to ensure that the glucose is completely dissolved. Tip into an ice-cream machine and churn until frozen. Stir in the finely chopped chilli, lime leaves and Malibu and tip the sorbet into a clean container and freeze until required.

To Serve: Lay the 6 pancakes out on a clean work surface. Spoon a generous amount of filling onto the centre of each pancake then fold in the sides to make a neat little parcel. Turn each parcel over and slice in half on the diagonal. Top with a scoop of sorbet and drizzle over the dark palm sugar syrup.

Serves 6

jasmine rice pudding
with toasted coconut ice-cream and lime syrup

Jasmine Rice Pudding

150 g (5 oz)
jasmine rice

15 g (¾ oz)
short grain rice

1 vanilla bean

900 ml (1½ pints) milk

90 g (3½ oz) caster
(superfine) sugar

3 egg yolks

90 g (3½ oz) unsalted
butter, softened

½ cup grated
palm sugar

Toasted Coconut Ice-Cream

140 g (5 oz)
threaded coconut

500 ml (16 fl oz) milk

350 ml (11½ fl oz)
thickened cream

8 egg yolks

170 g (6 oz) caster
(superfine) sugar

1½ tablespoons
Malibu

Lime Syrup

250 ml (7 fl oz) water

250 g (7 oz) caster
(superfine) sugar

zest and juice
of 2 limes

Garnish

6 large sprigs mint

When travelling through Thailand I tasted numerous versions of rice pudding – none of which were anything like the pudding I remembered from my childhood. Sadly, the quality and style of rice we grow here in Australia is very different from the earthiness and nuttiness of Thai or Indonesian rice, so it is hard to recreate the Asian style of rice-pudding. This is my interpretation, and is one of my favourite desserts – I love the intensity of the lime syrup with the smooth coconut ice-cream and creamy rice, and I particularly like the extra crunch that comes from the brulée topping.

Jasmine Rice Pudding: Rinse both types of rice in a colander under cold running water until the water runs clear. Place the rice in a heavy-based saucepan with the vanilla bean and milk. Bring to a gentle simmer, and cook for 16–18 minutes, stirring continuously to prevent the rice catching.

In a small bowl, mix the sugar and egg yolks together. Stir into the rice and cook gently for a further 5 minutes until the rice turns shiny and smooth. Remove from the heat, add the butter, stir well, and allow to cool. Line a baking tray with non-stick paper. Arrange 6 rings or moulds, 9 cm wide x 4 cm deep (3½ in x 1¾ in), on the baking tray and fill each one with rice pudding. Alternatively, spread the cooked rice mix over a tray (4 cm / 1¾ in deep) and use a cookie cutter to cut out the puddings once chilled. Place the tray in the fridge until the rice is set.

Toasted Coconut Ice-Cream: Preheat the oven to 180ºC (350ºF). Scatter the coconut on a baking sheet and toast in the oven for a few minutes until evenly browned. Put the toasted coconut into a saucepan with the milk and cream and simmer for 20 minutes to infuse.

In a bowl whisk together the eggs and sugar until they become thick and pale. Strain the warm milk onto the egg mixture and whisk vigorously. Place the bowl over a saucepan of simmering water. Heat gently for 5–10 minutes, stirring all the time, until the custard thickens enough to coat the back of a spoon. Place the bowl in a sink of iced water and allow to cool. Stir in the Malibu then pour the custard into an ice-cream machine and churn until frozen. Transfer the ice-cream into a clean container and place in the freezer until ready to serve.

Lime Syrup: Mix the water and sugar in a small non-reactive saucepan and heat until the sugar dissolves. Simmer gently until reduced by three-quarters. Brush the inside of the pan with water from time to time to stop it crystallising. To test if the syrup is ready, spoon a small amount onto a cold plate – it should be dense and sticky like treacle. Remove from the heat, stir in the lime juice and allow to cool. When the syrup is cold, stir in the lime zest and refrigerate until needed.

To Serve: Preheat your griller to its highest temperature. Remove the rice puddings from the refrigerator and transfer them onto a metal baking sheet. Lift off the moulds and sprinkle the top of each pudding with a thin layer of palm sugar. Place under the grill for a few moments until the sugar caramelises, then leave them to cool and the sugar to set hard. If you have a domestic blowtorch, this is even more effective.

Carefully transfer the rice puddings onto 6 plates, accompanied by a scoop of ice-cream. Drizzle a generous amount of lime syrup around each plate and garnish the puddings with a sprig of mint.

Serves 6

index